INDONESIA'S STRUGGLE
JEMAAH ISLAMIYAH AND THE SOUL OF ISLAM

Greg Barton is a senior lecturer in the School of Social and International Studies at Deakin University. A frequent commentator on Indonesian politics and Islam, he has written widely on these topics. He is the author of *Abdurrahman Wahid, Indonesian President, Muslim Democrat: A View from the Inside* (UNSW Press, 2002)

BRIEFINGS

A series of topical books exploring social, political
and cultural issues in contemporary Australia

Series editors: Peter Browne and Julian Thomas
Australian Policy Online (www.apo.org.au)
Institute for Social Research, Swinburne University of Technology

Also in this series

America's Pie: Trade and Culture Since 9/11
by Jock Given

Slapping on the Writs:
Defamation, Developers and Community Activism
by Brian Walters

Mr Ruddock Goes to Geneva
by Spencer Zifcak

Sexing It Up: Iraq, Intelligence and Australia
by Geoffrey Barker

Refuge Australia: Australia's Humanitarian Record
by Klaus Neumann

Rebels with a Cause: Independents in Australian Politics
by Brian Costar & Jennifer Curtin

The Case for an Australian Bill of Rights: Freedom in the War on Terror
by George Williams

The Politics of Medicare: Who Gets What, When and How
by Gwendolyn Gray

Indonesia's Struggle

JEMAAH ISLAMIYAH AND THE SOUL OF ISLAM

GREG BARTON

A UNSW Press book

Published by
University of New South Wales Press Ltd
University of New South Wales
Sydney NSW 2052
AUSTRALIA
www.unswpress.com.au

© Greg Barton 2004
First published 2004

This book is copyright. Apart from any fair dealing for the purpose of private study, research, criticism or review, as permitted under the Copyright Act, no part may be reproduced by any process without written permission. Enquiries should be addressed to the publisher.

National Library of Australia
Cataloguing-in-Publication entry

Barton, Greg, 1962– .

Indonesia's struggle: Jemaah Islamiyah and the soul of Islam.

ISBN 0 86840 759 3.

1. Jemaah Islamiyah (Organization). 2. Terrorism – Religious aspects – Islam. 3. Islamic fundamentalism – Asia, Southeastern. I. Title. (Series: Briefings series).

303.6250959

Edited by Carla Taines

Cover photograph: Irwin Fedriansyah / Associated Press
Printed by BPA Digital

Contents

1. The breakthrough — 7

2. Understanding radical Islamism — 25

3. Jemaah Islamiyah's struggle — 44

4. The political struggle — 63

5. Responding to radical Islamism — 76

Notes — 90

People mentioned in the text — 98

Glossary of terms and abbreviations — 112

Acknowledgements — 118

*For Siew Mee
and Hannah*

CHAPTER 1
The breakthrough

Could the Bali bombing have been avoided? Could Australian intelligence and security authorities have been expected to prevent the tragedy in Bali on 12 October 2002? The short answer appears to be no. In hindsight, we did not know as much as we should have about jihadi Islamist terrorists in Southeast Asia, and we failed to see the patterns in the information that we did have as clearly and as completely as we could and should have. But hindsight, precisely because of its wonderful clarity, is an unfair measure of reasonable expectations.

The really important questions to ask now are: what has been learned from the Bali bombing? Do we understand things now as fully as we should? Are we doing what is needed to prevent future tragedies? Do we know what we are up against?

In asking whether more could have been done to stop the Bali bombing we are overlooking a very important truth. It now seems certain that extremely good investigative work following the bombing, involving unprecedented international cooperation, has already prevented other similar tragedies. October 12 would likely have been but one of several bombing "spectaculars" in the region had the organisation behind the Bali bombing, Jemaah Islamiyah (JI), not been discovered and interrupted.

Many, many more lives could have been lost by now and the struggle against terrorism mired in mistrust, dysfunctional relationships and ignorance, were it not for the breakthrough in Bali. We are inclined to overlook how success in the Bali investigation so profoundly changed things. If we are to understand what we are up against now, we need to learn from Bali. We need to know how that breakthrough almost did not happen.

•

Three weeks after the Bali bombing the team of investigators led by senior police officer General I Made Mangku Pastika had almost completed an exhaustive examination of the bombsite and its environs. The forensic investigation was conducted by 400 Indonesian police (Polri) and 110 foreign investigators, mostly officers from the Australian Federal Police (AFP) under the command of Graham Ashton, but also including specialists from Scotland Yard and the US Federal Bureau of Investigation; it would run for 34 days. By Saturday 2 November, however, Pastika was beginning to despair. The investigation had begun well. Pastika's men were, in the main, not nearly as experienced as the foreign investigators in this sort of investigation but they were highly motivated and keen to learn. The fact that Ashton spoke Indonesian fluently and had a good personal rapport with Pastika, and that he understood the importance of playing a low-key role in this unprecedented joint endeavour, made it possible for the two teams to work well together. Early in the investigation it was agreed that the two teams would take their own independent samples and conduct separate analysis at the forensic laboratory established in the hotel they operated from in Bali, with samples being sent to Scotland Yard for further testing if results did not match. Ashton's team stressed the importance of establishing the sort of evidentiary trail that would stand up to rigorous questioning in court.

Pastika's men learnt quickly and by the end of the third week the investigators had assembled an impressive array of evidence. They were now fairly certain that the bomb used at the Sari Club was mainly made from the industrial chemical potassium chlorate and they had a good understanding of the mechanisms behind the bombings. Once they had made some arrests and could take fingerprints and DNA samples, they would be in a strong position to establish guilt. In such a position it was likely that the suspects, in detention and confronted with the forensic evidence pointing to their complicity, would quickly begin to talk. What they lacked, however, three weeks into the investigation, was the sort of breakthrough discovery that would lead them to their first arrest, and without that they looked like running up against a brick wall.

Ashton and Pastika were well aware that the investigation following the 1993 bombing of the World Trade Center in New York had achieved a breakthrough by linking serial numbers found on the mangled chassis of the truck used as a vehicle bomb with the bombers via the records of a truck rental firm. As their peers had done in New York nine years earlier, the investigators worked hard to locate and identify the fragments of wreckage from the vehicle bomb amid the debris of the bombsite. The engine block and various pieces of chassis from a 1983 Mitsubishi L300 minivan were located and scoured for identifying numbers. Two engineers from Mitsubishi in Japan were flown in to help. Unfortunately, at every place where a factory number should have been located there was evidence only of the number having being ground away. For a while it looked as if a complicated process of chemical washes might be able to restore sufficient traces of impressions from the stamping of a serial number to identify the vehicle. The process worked, but only partially, and not enough of the numbers could be identified to give them a lead.

A dejected Ashton returned briefly to Canberra to report to AFP commissioner Mick Keelty. Pastika turned to God. His colleagues knew Pastika, a Balinese Hindu, to be a man of principle and deeply religious so they were not surprised when he slipped out of the makeshift investigation centre and said that he was going to Besakih. Located high up on the south-western slopes of the sacred Mount Agung, the 3142-metre-high active volcano that dominates the Balinese landscape, the Besakih temple complex is the most important and sacred of Bali's many temple complexes. Pastika later recalled, "I had a feeling that we were missing something."

Back at the investigation centre, one of Pastika's colleagues felt himself drawn to look again at the twisted chassis rails that they had found lying on the roof of a building opposite the bombsite. Sharing his boss's frustration and disappointment, he stood gazing numbly at the blackened piece of wreckage that had promised so much yet had revealed so little. Suddenly it occurred to him that there was something odd about the assembly he was staring at. A piece of metal was joined to the main chassis rail with the sort of crude welding that suggested an improvised modification. Perhaps one of the vehicle's more recent owners had felt the need to reinforce the ageing structure. In itself this meant nothing – but what if there was something hidden under that plate? Seizing a hammer and cold chisel he set to work on the chassis and quickly dislodged the metal patch. There, on the chassis beam, was a stamped serial number. Putting down the tools, he picked up his mobile phone and dialled Pastika. "General, are you still praying?" "Yes, I'm still at the temple." "Well, you can come back now, your prayers have worked – I've just found a number on the chassis."

They had the breakthrough they needed. The serial number DPR15463 proved to be a Bali Transport Authority registration number. Apparently, the L300 van had served time as a minibus in Bali. A check of the records revealed that it had first been registered in Bali in 1987, and had had a long chain of owners since then. Within a day Polri investigators had followed the chain to the sixth owner on the list, a man in East Java, who told them how a man named Amrozi from the nearby district of Lamongan had approached him to purchase the minivan, explaining that he particularly wanted a vehicle with a Balinese registration plate and paying for it in Malaysian ringgit and US dollars. Within two days of the discovery of the stamped number, Pastika's men had Amrozi's house in the village of Tenggulun under surveillance. Early the next day Pastika gave the order to move in. Amrozi was asleep in the back of the house. He did not attempt to fight but instead began to laugh. He later exclaimed, "Gosh, you guys are very clever – how did you find me?"

Once Amrozi was arrested the rest of the pieces fell quickly into place. Apart from the increasingly talkative Amrozi the police also seized his mobile phone, complete with dozens of stored numbers and its electronic record of recent calls. When they searched Amrozi's workshop they found bags of bomb-making chemicals; soil samples from the area tested positive for traces of potassium chlorate, the main ingredient used in the Sari Club bomb. They also found a document with notes costing out the bombing and receipts for the purchase of large quantities of industrial chemicals from a shop in Surabaya. Inside his house they found training manuals on ambush techniques and numerous articles about jihad. They also found copies of 22 speeches, most of them concerned with jihad, by Osama bin Laden and JI co-founder Abu Bakar Ba'asyir.

Amrozi began talking almost immediately and gave the police the names of six people he said were fellow members of his bomb team: Imam Samudra, Ali Imron, Dul Matin, Idris, Umar Patek and Abdul Ghani. Amrozi was not, however, telling the police everything he knew. He sought to conceal the name of two others, Zulkarnaen and his own much-revered older brother Mukhlas, despite naming his younger brother Ali Imron.

Initially, Amrozi's mobile phone revealed even more than did Amrozi. His arrest was kept secret for two days; when it was announced on 7 November the Polri–AFP team carefully monitored the sudden flurry of communications that took place between numbers recorded in Amrozi's phone before the chatter abruptly stopped. In a number of cases the calls were long enough for the investigators to locate the position of the phones and they closed in for a series of arrests. By acting quickly, they were able to outwit many of their suspects. On one occasion a large team of plain-clothes policemen were positioned in a village in Central Java ready to seize one of Amrozi's associates but, not being sure of what he looked like, they were fearful that he might slip through their net once they began questioning locals and he became aware of their presence. They resorted to a simple ruse and dialled the suspect's mobile phone. An undercover officer heard it ringing from the pocket of a young man standing near him and grabbed the suspect before he had any idea of what was happening.

Once Amrozi had been taken into custody and he, and his mobile phone, had begun to talk, the team realised that Imam Samudra was the likely mastermind behind the bombing. Capturing Samudra became their first priority. Tracking him down was not easy, however, for he was too smart to continue using the mobile phone number known to Amrozi. In mid-November they got lucky. While monitoring email traffic thought likely to be linked to Samudra, they found a message giving a mobile phone number. By tracking transmissions to that number they were able to intercept a number of mobile phone text messages. Samudra had avoided making phone calls precisely because he feared that voice calls would reveal his location. What he didn't realise was that the AFP had equipment sensitive enough to zero in on even a very brief text transmission. Samudra's last message revealed him to be in the port city of Merak in West Java, the departure point for ferries to Sumatra. The Polri–AFP team sent more than 30 police officers to Merak. An alert officer noticed a man with a cap slipped over his face slumped down in his seat at the back of a bus. Samudra struggled when approached but, trapped in the back of the bus, he could not escape. As well as his mobile phone he was also carrying a laptop computer that contained much valuable information. The contents of the hard drive, including deleted files, were examined by AFP technical experts who discovered pictures of Ba'asyir and of the burnt bodies of victims of the Bali bombing, along with the text of a statement Samudra had posted on a website claiming responsibility for the bombing. Another statement written for the website www.istimata.com gave an insight into Samudra's understanding of the struggle that he was involved in:

> Our demand, while troops and their allies America, England, Germany, Australia, France, Holland, Italy, Japan, Sweden, etc. do not pull out of Afghanistan, victims from your countries everywhere will continue to fall...
>
> While you all regard us as terrorists and you torture us in your prisons, especially in Guantanamo, citizens from your countries will feel the same thing.

Within hours of being taken into police custody in Jakarta Samudra had begun to talk, confessing to his role in the bombing in Bali the previous month. Interestingly, although he freely admitted to his role in the bombing and talked about other things, he was not willing to discuss what he knew about JI.

With Samudra and most of the other bombers now in custody, uncovering the JI network was of utmost priority if further bombings were to be avoided. Within hours of the bombing on 12 October, suspicion had already turned to JI. For weeks beforehand US and Australian authorities had been worried that a major terrorist strike was imminent and that it would most likely involve JI.

Two months before the bombing, the Jakarta office of the well-regarded think-tank the International Crisis Group (ICG), led by human rights activist Sidney Jones, published a 24-page report, *Al-Qaeda in Southeast Asia: The Case of the "Ngruki Network" in Indonesia*. Alongside what we now know about JI (including the information in the ICG's 46-page report of August 2003, *Jemaah Islamiyah in South East Asia: Damaged but Still Dangerous*), the August 2002 report is rather sketchy, focusing more on history than current activities. Nevertheless, the report was remarkably prescient at the time. It opens by observing that:

> One network of militant Muslims has produced all the Indonesian nationals so far suspected of links to al-Qaeda...
>
> The network has as its hub a religious boarding school (*pesantren* or *pondok*) near Solo, Central Java, known as Pondok Ngruki, after the village where the school is located...
>
> Most members of the network share common characteristics: loyalty to Pondok Ngruki or its founders; commitment to carrying on the struggle of Darul Islam rebellions of the 1950s; desire to create an Islamic state by first establishing an Islamic community or *jemaah islamiyah*, and shared experiences of political detention in the 1980s. Many are on the executive committee of an organisation formed in Yogyakarta in 2000 called the *Majelis Mujahidin Indonesia* (MMI, Indonesian Mujahidin Council).

The ICG report charts the development of the Ngruki network from its roots in the Darul Islam movement for an Islamic State of Indonesia (Negara Islam Indonesia, or NII) in West Java and Southern Sulawesi in the 1950s. It describes how two Islamic teachers, Abdullah Sungkar and Abu Bakar Ba'asyir, though not directly connected with the movement, took up the cause of establishing an Islamic state in the 1970s. The men met in Solo in 1963 and became close, life-long friends, working together on *dakwah* (mission) activities and in 1971 founding Pesantren al-Mukmin or, as it was known following its relocation in 1973 to the village of Ngruki on the outskirts of Solo, Pondok Ngruki. The pair was arrested in 1978 and charged on the basis of their association with Darul Islam–NII leader Hispan (Haji Ismail Pranoto) who had been detained the previous year. They were accused of having being inducted into Darul Islam by Hispan, under oath, in 1976 and of setting up an exclusivist "Islamic community" – literally, a *jemaah Islamiyah* – as a precursor to establishing an Islamic state. They finally faced court in 1982 and were sentenced to nine years in prison. But at the end of the year they were released, their sentences having being reduced to the equivalent of the time they had already spent in detention. The prosecution appealed against the reduced sentences but Sungkar and Ba'asyir were able to return to Pondok Ngruki and to their struggle to make Indonesia truly Islamic by setting up small exclusivist communities (*jemaah*) and cells (*usrah*) after the model of Hassan al-Banna, founder of Egypt's Muslim Brotherhood. The next two years witnessed a resurgence of interest in Darul Islam–style radical Islamism in Solo and in the university city of Yogyakarta an hour to the south, partly inspired by the success of the Islamic revolution in Iran in 1979.

Sungkar and Ba'asyir worked closely in Yogyakarta with radical Islamist *muballigh* (preachers) such as Abu Jibril, his brother Irfan Awwas and Agus Dwikarna. Awwas had come to prominence in the student community for his bold reporting of the Sungkar–Ba'asyir trial; he was arrested in 1983 and sentenced to thirteen years' detention on charges of subversion.

In February 1985, when the prosecution appeal was upheld in the Indonesian Supreme Court, Abdullah Sungkar and Abu Bakar Ba'asyir decided to flee to Malaysia. There they were free to continue the struggle and began to turn their attention to recruiting *mujahidin* (fighters in a holy war, or jihad) to join the resistance against the Soviets in Afghanistan. They were joined in Malaysia by an inner circle of colleagues and Ngruki graduates including Amrozi, his brother Mukhlas (graduated from Ngruki in 1982), Zulkarnaen (graduated from Ngruki in 1979), Abu Jibril (who was arrested by Malaysian authorities in June 2001 because of his activities in JI), Fathur Rahman al-Ghozi (graduated from Ngruki in 1989, and jailed in Manila in January 2002 for possession of explosives), Dul Matin (a regular visitor to Ngruki), along with Ali Imron, Hambali, Abdullah Ansori and Imam Samudra. Thoriqudin (believed to have replaced Ba'asyir as *amir* of JI following Ba'asyir's arrest after the Bali bombing) was intermittently involved in this group. In time they were also joined by Malaysian recruits such as Faiz Abu Bakar Bafana, his brother Fathi Abu Bakar Bafana and Wan Min bin Wan Mat.

It was during this exile in Malaysia in the 1990s that the formal organisation of JI began to take shape. From 1995 Sungkar and Ba'asyir apparently became even further radicalised through their contact with the Middle Eastern group Gama Islami (the name is a variant transliteration of *jemaah Islamiyah*), one of al-Qaeda's key associates. It appears that this association with Gama Islami helped expand their vision to a more global perspective.

Nevertheless, for Abdullah Sungkar and Abu Bakar Ba'asyir the concept behind the struggle they were engaged in had long been much greater than a merely local, Southeast Asian one. In fact, Sungkar, Ba'asyir and colleagues in the Darul Islam–NII network had began conscripting their followers to join the jihad in Afghanistan as early as 1985. Abdullah Ansori had been specially tasked with attracting more *mujahidin* to join the struggle. Most of the funding for the Southeast Asian recruits came from the Saudi-backed Muslim World League, "the Rabitah" (from Rabitat al-Alam al Islami); their training in Pakistan and Afghanistan was at the hands of Osama bin Laden's close associates, Abdullah Azzam and Abdul Rasul Sayyaf, through whom they met bin Laden.

Among the many JI members who fought and studied in Afghanistan or Pakistan (or both) were Dul Matin, Dr Azahari Husin, Hambali, Zulkarnaen, Mukhlas, Ali Imron, Fathur Rahman al-Ghozi, Faiz Abu Bakar Bafana and Fathi Abu Bakar Bafana. Indeed, virtually all of JI's senior leadership had spent time in Afghanistan, most of them returning to Southeast Asia before 1992 when JI was formally constituted.

Sungkar and Ba'asyir returned to Indonesia and to Pondok Ngruki immediately after the Soeharto regime fell in May 1998. Sungkar died of natural causes shortly afterwards and (according to JI detainees such as Faiz Abu Bakar Bafana) Abu Bakar Ba'asyir was made *amir*, or spiritual head, of JI in his place. The *amir* holds an important position of authority because in radical Islamist organisations such as al-Qaeda, Darul Islam and JI the core members of the organisation must swear an oath of loyalty and obedience (*bayyat*) to the *amir*.

Ba'asyir and his followers enjoyed much greater freedom in post-Soeharto Indonesia and they made good use of it. One of their initiatives was to establish the Indonesian Mujahidin Council (Majelis

Mujahidin Indonesia – MMI). The ostensible purpose of MMI was to bring together all of the groups in Indonesia working for the application of Shariah, or Islamic law. The first congress of MMI was held in Solo in August 2000. President Abdurrahman Wahid was concerned about the meeting but, as campaigning for the application of Shariah was a perfectly legitimate activity, there was nothing that a democratically elected president could do to stop it. Nevertheless, many observers felt deeply uneasy about MMI at the time of its inauguration and this unease only deepened in the wake of the Bali bombing. The senior leadership of MMI is filled with familiar names from JI and affiliated militant Islamist organisations, including Abu Bakar Ba'asyir (Amir ul-Mujahidin), Agus Dwikarna (general secretary), Irfan Awwas (head of executive committee) and Abu Jibril (executive committee member).

A little over a month after the ICG report on the Ngruki network was published, an issue of *Time* magazine confirmed the worst fears of many observers. The lead story was entitled "Confessions of an al-Qaeda Terrorist: American interrogators finally got to Omar al-Faruq, who detailed plans to launch a new terror spree in Southeast Asia." Heavily reliant on CIA documents, and for this reason immediately dismissed by many in Indonesia and quite a few experts outside Indonesia, the story purported to set forth the substance of Omar al-Faruq's long-awaited confession to US authorities.

Time reported that Omar al-Faruq was born in Kuwait in 1971 and had spent three years training with al-Qaeda in Khaldan, Afghanistan, during which time he became close to camp leader al-Mughira al-Gaza'iri and to Abu Zubaydah, a senior associate of Osama bin Laden. In 1995, at a time when al-Qaeda was very active in the Philippines, al-Faruq travelled with al-Mughira to Camp Abubakar in Mindanao, using a false Philippines passport. Several years later, in the wake of Soeharto's resignation as president, he left the Moro Islamic Liberation Front terrorist training camp and travelled south by boat to the Indonesian island of Sulawesi to coordinate al-Qaeda's Southeast Asian campaign. There he married an Indonesian woman and linked up with Agus Dwikarna in the port city of Makassar in the former Darul Islam stronghold of South Sulawesi. Because he was unsuccessful in mastering Indonesian he was not able to use an Indonesian passport, something that was to cause him trouble when immigration authorities detained him in mid-2001. Nevertheless, al-Faruq was able to slip away, and he relocated to the small town of Cijeruk, West Java, an hour's drive from Jakarta.

On 25 February 2002, according to *Time*, the CIA informed Indonesian intelligence authorities that three Indonesian-based militant Islamists had established a training camp on the island of Borneo. Indonesian intelligence officers discovered that four MMI members, including al-Faruq and Dwikarna, had been involved in training terrorists at the camp. Weeks later, the Philippine police arrested Dwikarna at Manila airport; they found al-Faruq's number in his mobile phone. In April 2002 Zubaydah was captured in Faisalabad, Pakistan. His phone also had al-Faruq's number. So did the phone of an al-Qaeda agent detained in Guantanamo Bay. The CIA discovered that Fathur Rahman al-Ghozi had also been phoning al-Faruq, as had the al-Qaeda-linked Chechen leader Ibin al-Khattab. On 23 May Zubaydah was shown a photograph of al-Faruq and confessed that the man in the photograph was his al-Qaeda associate "al-Faruq al Kuwait." Within two weeks al-Faruq was arrested by Indonesian authorities and handed over to the Americans for interrogation with the consent of coordinating security minister, Susilo Bambang Yudhoyono.

Omar al-Faruq was detained on 6 May 2002 but he did not start opening up to his interrogators until 9 September 2002. For more than three months al-Faruq was subject to a battery of psychological interrogation techniques, including periods of sleep deprivation and solitary confinement. Once he did begin to talk, al-Faruq proved to be a rich vein of information. Confirming what the Americans had already been told by Abu Zubaydah, he confessed that he reported to Zubaydah as coordinator of al-Qaeda activities in Southeast Asia. He went on to detail his activities in Southeast Asia and make the alarming claim that Zubaydah had ordered him to "plan large-scale attacks against US interests in Indonesia, Malaysia, [the] Philippines, Singapore, Thailand, Taiwan, Vietnam and Cambodia." The CIA report of al-Faruq's confession explained that he had "prepared a plan to conduct simultaneous car and truck bomb attacks against US embassies in the region" around the time of the September 11 anniversary. As soon as the confession had been made, a report was sent to the CIA

Counterterrorism Center in Langley, Virginia. The centre, which had already been receiving reports of increased electronic signals chatter and of suspicious activities in the vicinity of US embassies in the region, moved quickly to issue a code-orange alert.

The *Time* article claimed that as early as 1999 al-Faruq had begun planning a series of audacious attacks on high-profile figures in Indonesia but had failed to put any of them into action. When it appeared, the article was widely discredited for its account of a second plan to assassinate Megawati Sukarnoputri (before she became president), which failed because the small bomb being carried by Megawati's would-be assassin blew up prematurely in the Atrium Mall in Central Jakarta. Incredibly, the bomber did not die in the blast but merely lost a leg. Indonesian observer Harold Crouch wryly remarked that it would obviously take a much bigger bomb than that to take out Megawati. Much more credible was the claim that al-Faruq had told the CIA he had helped Dwikarna to establish the radical Islamist militia Laskar Jundullah in South Sulawesi, a group now known to have significantly exacerbated inter-communal violence in the Poso region of Central Sulawesi.

Omar al-Faruq was reported to have confessed to masterminding the Christmas Eve bombings in 2000 in churches across Indonesia – incidents that led to the deaths of eighteen people and injured more than 100. He had apparently "cased the US Embassy in Jakarta to develop a plan to destroy the embassy with a large car bomb," only to abandon the plan when it became clear that tightened security made this unfeasible.

Although much of al-Faruq's confession merely served to corroborate earlier suspicions, his claims about Abu Bakar Ba'asyir challenged preconceptions. It had been assumed that, as *amir*, Ba'asyir was merely the spiritual leader of JI and that it was Hambali who ran JI's terrorist operations. The CIA report of al-Faruq's interrogation, summarised in *Time*, painted a rather different picture. According to the magazine:

> The CIA report states that Abubakar Ba'asyir, 64, the cleric who is the alleged spiritual leader of JI, "authorized Faruq to use JI operatives and resources to conduct" the embassy bombings planned for last week:

al-Faruq told the CIA that Ba'asyir dispatched a JI member named Abu al-Furkan to oversee a planned attack on the U.S. Embassy in Malaysia. Al-Faruq said Ba'asyir was also behind a 1999 bombing of Jakarta's largest mosque and then blamed Christians for the act…

While intelligence officials have long believed that Hambali ran the day-to-day operations of JI, al-Faruq told the CIA that Ba'asyir was just as eager to work with al-Qaeda, even dispatching his aides to procure weapons and explosives for al-Faruq and his cronies. Last week Ba'asyir repeated his longstanding denial of connection with terrorist groups. "I don't have any link whatsoever with al-Qaeda," he told TIME, "but if al-Qaeda's struggle is for the best interest of Islam, I support it."

When the issue of *Time* appeared in mid-September it was greeted with scepticism by many Islamists, a number of western observers and even some moderate Muslim leaders. It clearly embarrassed the Megawati administration, which was extremely reluctant to admit that in JI it had a problem with al-Qaeda-linked terrorism of the magnitude suggested by the *Time* report. Predictably, the article infuriated Abu Bakar Ba'asyir and moved him to instruct his lawyers to sue the magazine. (He also decided to sue the Singaporean government for its comments about what JI detainees had allegedly said about his complicity in JI terror planning.)

The fact that the allegations about JI and about Ba'asyir were being dismissed by Indonesian officials as senior as vice-president Hamzah Haz does not mean, however, that the Indonesian investigators working with Pastika were ignoring the mounting evidence against JI. From the outset Pastika and Ashton had worked towards collecting forensic evidence of a quality and range that would withstand harsh examination. They were working from the ground up and were not primarily driven by intelligence analysis. Nevertheless, once a solid evidentiary link had been established between the bomb vehicle and Amrozi, and they had many of the bombers in custody, they knew that they were well on the way not only to solving the crime of 12 October but also to disrupting JI's operations through a series of arrests that would lead to the permanent removal of terrorists from the field.

One of the keys to getting detainees to cooperate was confronting them with an array of forensic evidence so substantial that they knew that denial of guilt was pointless. Graham Ashton's approach to the investigation was clear from the start:

> The most important things to establish at a bombing scene is the vehicle used, along with the device that detonated it, the container that held the device and what the bomb itself was made of. These are important because once you have discovered these things they are traceable. As are the people that bought them. You can find receipts, sales staff that remember selling things to people and what those people looked like. That is the sort of corroborative evidence you need to make a case stick. I was asked repeatedly early on to say who I thought was responsible for the bombing. My answer was always the same – and that was that there was no point in speculating as the physical evidence would lead us to the perpetrators. It's the evidentiary trail that leads you to a suspect, and that's exactly what happened in this case.

The painstaking approach taken by investigators searching for data within the 40,000-square-metre crime scene steadily yielded results. An early breakthrough came when investigators were able to establish that the primary explosive material used in the blast was the inexpensive and readily available industrial cleaning agent potassium chlorate. The Indonesian team was initially sceptical; such was the scale of the devastation that they thought the blast had been driven by RDX, a military-issue, high-velocity, plastic explosive. If that had proven to be the case it would have pointed a finger of suspicion at groups such as Laskar Jihad known to have good military connections, as RDX is not readily available outside military agencies. The trouble with pursuing the potassium chlorate hypothesis was that the chemical is highly water-soluble and the bombsite had been thoroughly hosed down before it was declared a crime scene and sealed off. AFP officers were eventually able to recover small amounts of potassium chlorate from the leaves of trees, the mangled wreck of an electricity pole and even from the bottom of the water-filled bomb crater where it was preserved in clumps of bituminised road surface fused together by the blast. Once their hunch about the composition of the Sari Club bomb had been proven correct they knew that, contrary to the general line of suspicion that had followed previous bombings in Indonesia, they were more likely to be dealing with al-Qaeda-style terrorists than with state-linked militias or rogue military elements.

The care taken in collecting samples, often only a millimetre or two in diameter, led investigators to conclude that the small, symbolic bomb that exploded outside the US consulate at Denpasar at about the same time as the main Bali bombs was detonated by a cheap Nokia 5110 mobile phone, and that the bombing of Paddy's Bar was the work of a suicide bomber.

The Polri–AFP team was disciplined and hard-working, but they also had some luck. Apart from the main breakthrough in finding the hidden transport authority registration number on the L300 chassis rail, and thus establishing a link with Amrozi, several other breaks helped them establish a watertight prosecution case.

The great strength of Islamist terrorism is its power to persuade young men to freely give up their lives for "the struggle." One of its concomitant weaknesses, however, is that the majority of dedicated young men who become "foot soldiers of the revolution" are enthusiastic amateurs. Fortunately, Amrozi had not stolen the bomb vehicle but had foolishly paid (and in foreign currency at that!) for the L300 minivan, leaving him traceable. The getaway motorcycle used by the bombers was also traceable.

Incredibly, Amrozi, Idris and Ali Imron had simply walked into a dealer and bought a brand new Yamaha FZ1R after enquiring how much they could resell it for if they brought it back several days later. Imron used the bike to drop off the small initial bomb outside the US consulate. Idris then rode the bike as Imron drove suicide bombers Jimi and Iqbal to Jalan Legian in Kuta. He stopped 400 metres from the Sari Club, instructed Iqbal to don his explosive vest and Jimi to arm the vehicle bomb, and then left Jimi, who had never learnt to drive and could only drive in a straight line, to complete his journey. Idris picked up Imron on the bike and the pair headed back into Denpasar as Idris dialled the number of the Nokia 5110 that was to detonate the bomb outside the US consulate. Ali Imron and Idris left the Yamaha in the yard of a mosque where it attracted the attention of the caretaker. He had been sleeping but had been woken by the explosions in Jalan Legian and was watching when Ali Imron and Idris rode in, parked the bike and left, leaving a pair of gloves and two helmets with the bike. Curious, he later walked over to inspect the motorcycle and noticed the three electrical cut-off switches that Ali Imron had fitted the day before. Thinking that the bike might be connected with the bombing, he contacted the police.

The Indonesian police were also suspicious and worked quickly to identify the shop from which the bike had been purchased. Not surprisingly, staff in the shop remembered the odd trio who had paid cash for the bike, and were even able to provide descriptions that were sufficiently detailed to enable a local artist to sketch three likenesses. At this point a specialist team from Melbourne skilled in using sophisticated photo-fit software was brought in to develop the photo likenesses that soon appeared in the media. Indonesian police had no trouble recognising Amrozi when they arrived at his home.

With most of the bombers in detention, attention turned to ensuring that the evidence for the prosecution was as complete as possible. The arrest of Ali Imron in January 2003 provided another vital link as he was able to guide them to the house in Denpasar used to assemble the bomb. Significantly, Ali Imron was the only one of the bombers to exhibit apparent remorse over the loss of lives caused by the bombing and thus was the only bomber seen to fully cooperate with his interrogators. Police had earlier located several other properties used by the bombers in Bali but had not been able to locate the "bomb factory." Now they had one final lucky break. AFP director of counter-terrorism Tim Morris explained:

> We had already been told by our counterparts in the Metropolitan Police, who had been investigating the IRA for 30 years, how vital it is to find the bomb factory, as they call it. Such bomb factories yield a mountain of vital evidence and Imron took us right to it. He told us exactly how the Sari Club bomb was built, what was in it and who assembled it.

Remarkably, although it had been three months since the bombers had been there, the house had remained empty, and Polri–AFP forensic investigators were able to collect a wealth of valuable material. They found traces of potassium chlorate and other bomb-making chemicals such as PETN (used in detonating cord) throughout the house, including on a toilet seat and a ladle in the bathroom. Tyre tracks consistent with a Mitsubishi L300 were found in the garage. DNA in earwax on a cotton bud was found to match that of Mukhlas. Fingerprints matching those of bomber Abdul Ghani were found on the back door; other fingerprints found on the garage door frame and a rear living room window were found to match those of the bomb-builder, Sawad. A footprint on a copy of the *Bali Post* found in one of the Bali houses used by the bombers proved a perfect match for Amrozi's right foot. When the bombers finally appeared in court in mid-2003 the evidence arrayed against them was comprehensive and compelling.

•

Revulsion at the bombings and revelations about the violent intentions of previously respected radical Islamist leaders greatly reduced sympathy for radical Islamism among Indonesians. Ironically, however, the unprecedented effectiveness of the police investigators left even moderate Islamic leaders openly sceptical of official pronouncements about JI. It has to be remembered that Indonesians were still not accustomed to rapid and effective police work. Many people found it difficult to accept that the rapid succession of arrests and new evidence was based on professional police work. The involvement of foreign police officers further complicated perceptions. Nevertheless, the breakthrough in linking Amrozi with the Mitsubishi L300 minivan used in the bombing of the Sari Club, and the arrests and confessions that flowed from this, were instrumental in turning public opinion against JI and radical Islamism. This was reinforced by the fact that the Bali trials were widely perceived to have been unusually transparent and professional.

In virtually every respect the prosecution of the Bali bombers was a model of how justice in Indonesia can serve the interests of ordinary Indonesians in a liberal democracy. The main weakness in the prosecution was that the bombers were charged under anti-terrorism legislation introduced after the bombings. Because a recent amendment to the Indonesian constitution had made retrospective legislation invalid except in the case of an extraordinary crime, the prosecution was always vulnerable to legal challenge. The new Constitutional Court's five-to-four vote on 23 July 2004 that the legislation could not be applied retrospectively to the Bali bombing should therefore have come as no surprise. Nor should such an outcome be viewed as a failure of law – on the contrary, distressing circumstances aside, the emergence of a vigorously independent Constitutional Court defending the constitution should be seen as a positive development.

Nevertheless, the reasoning behind the court's decision is disturbing. Writing in the *Jakarta Post* on 3 August, American academic Jeffery Winters pointed out that the nine justices were not debating the issue of retrospectivity, on which they were all agreed, but rather whether or not the Bali bombing represented an "extraordinary crime." The judges who thought it did included the only two members of the court with international legal training. Four of the five judges in the majority (in particular Chief Justice Jimmly Asshidique) are known to have radical Islamist sympathies and the fifth judge comes from the military. They argued that, terrible though it was, the loss of hundreds of lives in the attack in Bali was no more terrible than the loss of thousands of Muslim lives in communal violence over the past five years, and so the Bali bombing could not be construed as an "extraordinary crime."

The shock waves sent around the world by the September 11 terrorist strikes in 2001 were felt no less strongly in Indonesia than they were in other Muslim countries, but it was the 12 October bombing in Bali in 2002 that really shook up the world's largest Muslim country. In this largely pro-western nation both attacks were met with waves of sympathy. Whereas the September 11 attacks, awful though they were, seemed a long way off, the 12 October bombing confronted Indonesia with the horrible reality that global terrorism was its problem too – a problem it now had to deal with at home.

The events of 12 October challenged our understanding of Indonesian Islam. The conventional wisdom for decades has been that Islam in the "Malay world" of Southeast Asia generally, and especially in Indonesia, is quintessentially different from the Islam of Pakistan and the Arab world – countries where Islamist extremists intimidate otherwise secular governments into supporting their demands and allowing them the final say in how Islam is interpreted. This view holds that radical Islamism will never be a serious political force in Indonesia and that extremists constitute such a small proportion of Indonesia's 200 million Muslims as to be no significant threat. The bombing in Bali and the subsequent discovery that it was the work of local activists linked to Jemaah Islamiyah, itself linked to al-Qaeda, have challenged this view.

CHAPTER 2
Understanding radical Islamism

This short book aims to provide a contextualised understanding of Indonesian Islamism in all its forms, and to offer an objective assessment of the risk Islamist radicalism presents to the social and political stability of the region. Only a global and interdisciplinary approach – an approach that pays equal attention to ideas, to actions and to context – will help us to understand Islam and Islamism. This book reviews the changes that have taken place in Indonesian Islam over the past three decades and examines their social and political context in order to assess the extent to which radical Islamists and progressive liberals, representing as they do small minorities at each end of the broad spectrum of Indonesian Islam, are able to act as catalysts for social and political change. And while I counsel against undue alarmism I also argue against complacency and for the need to take both radical Islamism and Islam itself more seriously. The book concludes by discussing the implications for domestic and international policy and looking at how moderate Islamic groups can be helped to strengthen civil society.

Too much of the commentary in the media about Islamist terrorism, in relation to both Indonesia and the wider Muslim world, has been simplistic and superficial. The truth is seldom neat and simple, and if we are to apprehend it we need to get below the surface. To effectively engage with this subject, especially if we hope to anticipate and influence future developments, requires a multidimensional approach that gives careful attention to three discrete elements. Any sound understanding of the current reality must rest evenly on each of these three legs: the seminal ideas; the pattern of history; and the contemporary context.

The remainder of this chapter is devoted to an examination of the seminal ideas behind radical Islamism in general and Jemaah Islamiyah in particular. Chapter 3 reviews the history of JI, beginning with its roots in the Darul Islam movement in the 1950s through to the present. Chapter 4 examines the contemporary social and political context and synergies between jihadi Islamism and political Islamism. Finally, chapter 5 looks at how the seminal ideas, the pattern of history and the contemporary context shape current and future developments, and examines the policy implications for responding to radical Islamism.

•

Judging by appearances is seldom a good idea. When it comes to religion, it is a particularly inept strategy. We are likely either to equate difference with danger, and become prejudicial, or to be captured by the exotic, and become naive and uncritical. To interpret the traditional Islamic dress and manner of the Acehnese as indicative of religious extremism, for example, would be a foolish error. To then link this, as some in the international media have done, with the Acehnese struggle for self-determination, and paint it as religious conflict, is an even graver error, one that blinds us to the real issues and the underlying problems of injustice, human rights abuses and military brutality.

Traditionally, the study of ideas in the Muslim world has been left to orientalists, or text-oriented experts, whose careful scholarly approach has often not extended to a consideration of social and political engagement and the real-world application of the documents they are studying. At the same time, comparatively few political scientists and commentators have a deep knowledge of the religious thought associated with the groups they are observing, and frequently all political parties or groups with an Islamic connection are lumped together. And, if it is rare to find a writer who makes an effort to understand both the mindsets and the political activism of these groups, it is even rarer to find someone who links this knowledge to an awareness of the changing political and social context in which the groups operate.

Ironically, one of the main reasons why the west puts so little effort into understanding the central ideas of Islamic groups appears to be that coming to grips with those ideas seems too difficult. Much of the time we are not even sure quite what we mean by "Islam," much less how we can objectively evaluate its various forms. Consider for a moment the expressions we use: "political Islam," "Indonesian Islam," the "role of Islam," the "Islamic influence," the "Islamic factor" and so forth. We understand, of course, that while Islam is a deeply personal faith for many believers, for others there is no separating faith and politics. In any case, regardless of one's view of secularisation and modernisation, there is a very real sense in which Islam is nothing less than the sum total of a raft of social, cultural and political norms, expectations, convictions, values, habits, traditions, outlooks, attitudes and identity markers.

While there are good reasons for saying that Islam is all of these things, we cannot progress in our analysis if we only talk in generalities. Without greater precision in our language we risk endlessly groping for direction in a fog of confusion. Ludwig Wittgenstein famously observed that many philosophical problems are the result of "language going on holidays." The same observation could well be made concerning religion. Wittgenstein also offered a solution to a deficit of clear thinking —pay particular attention to the identification of "family likenesses" – and that is as good an argument as any for persisting with trying to find appropriate categories and terminology.

Many Muslims living in the west have experienced an increase in aggressive Islamophobia in the wake of the September 11 attacks, and many have suffered humiliation, or worse, as a result of heightened security regimes. And Muslims around the world have cringed at the way in which Islam and Muslims are so often depicted in the western media. It is understandable, then, that many Muslims question the appropriateness of using expressions such as "Islamic terrorism." Nevertheless, the fact that many terrorists and militant extremists see themselves to be acting in the interests of Islam cannot be denied. We need a way of talking about these very real problems that avoids the fallacy of essentialism and produces the maximum of light with the minimum of heat.

A good starting point in our effort to analyse and categorise Islamic movements and political parties is to examine the beliefs, ideas and ideologies by which these groups define themselves.

One of the most helpful and accurate terms to emerge in recent years is that of "Islamism." Islamists, or those who hold to Islamism, believe that Islam can and should form the basis of political ideology. Handled with sensitivity, the term "Islamism" is one that both insiders and outsiders can relate to with a reasonable degree of common understanding. That is considerably more than can be said of terms like "fundamentalism" and "radicalism," both of which tend to be ambiguous. Islamism covers a broad spectrum of convictions. At one extreme are those who would merely like to see Islam accorded proper recognition in national life in terms of national symbols. At the other extreme are those who want to see the radical transformation of society and politics, by whatever means, into an absolute theocracy (which, in practice, involves the rule of clerics). Here the word "radical" is used in its original sense to denote profound change from the "roots" up (the Latin word for root is "radix" and it is from this that we get "radical").

While Islamists find in Islam something of a blueprint for political engagement, non-Islamist Muslims find nothing more specific than values and principles. A significant minority, however, find in these core values of Islam a counter-argument to Islamism. They argue that not only should Islam be first and foremost a personal faith, but it should also accept and respect differences of opinion, commitment and practice. They embrace terms such as "liberal" and "progressive," fully aware of connotations of these terms in post-enlightenment western thought. Where Islamists tend, to varying degrees, to problematise the relationship between Islam and western conceptions of modernity, liberal Islamic intellectuals find an essential congruity between western Judeo-Christian thought and Islam.

Liberals are comfortable articulating their political vision in terms of western concepts such as democracy, human rights, modernisation and the separation of "church" and state. Islamists, on the other hand, tend to draw more selectively on such ideas and instead argue that society will overcome the problems of modern life only when it becomes truly Islamic. To this end Islamists tend to place great stock in legislative reforms that commit the state to taking an interest in the Islamisation of society and, in particular, many see the implementation of Islamic law, or the Shariah, as a panacea for society's ills. In its most extreme forms Islamism is radical, revolutionary and utopian.

Some might question whether it is even appropriate to talk of radical Islamism posing a threat. Terrorism may be a threat but only a small minority of radical Islamists are terrorists, so why should all radical Islamists be tarred with the same brush? In dealing with these questions it is important to stress that religious conservatism – sometimes erroneously called "fundamentalism" – is not inherently bad. There are plenty of conservative, sometimes very conservative, religious traditions around the world that, for all their lack of appeal to outsiders, cannot fairly be said to be doing great harm. In fact, it could well be argued that the world is a richer place for their presence. The Amish of North America, for example, take an extremely conservative approach to Christianity but their conservatism does no harm to any outside their community. They are legalistic and have strong convictions but they are not about changing the broader society to conform with their convictions. There are many conservative Muslim communities that display similar characteristics and, like the Amish, they might sometimes be referred to as fundamentalist (even if, like the Amish, they could more accurately be described as hyper-conservative traditionalists).

Most scholars agree that fundamentalism is essentially a reaction to modernity. In this sense, fundamentalist groups – be they Christian, Jewish, Muslim or Hindu – are, despite their own sense of themselves, products of the modern era and generally have their origins in the late nineteenth and early twentieth centuries.

Islamism, however, means something quite different from this sort of "fundamentalism." Islamism is a response to modernity that has transformed the religion of Islam into a political ideology. Islamism is therefore pre-eminently concerned with changing society and political institutions in order to bring both the state and society into conformity with an understanding of Islam. Among other things, this involves formalising the state's constitutional and legislative recognition of Islam and, for radical Islamists, introducing the Shariah or Islamic law.

The problem with radical Islamism is that it seeks to impose a "tyranny" of a minority over the majority and is unconcerned about trespassing on the rights of others. This is not to say that radical Islamism is essentially a malevolent force. Rather, in attempting to have God's law applied in society, radical Islamists see themselves as being involved in a benevolent struggle to force society to take the only medicine that can cure it of its ills. And if the majority of people cannot see this, then it only proves that society is blinded by its illness. Radical Islamists thus act in the spirit of theocracy rather than democracy but nevertheless believe that they are working for the greater good. In practice, aggressive legalism and the application of a narrow understanding of the Shariah can lead to serious erosion of human rights, especially those of women and of the poor and the weak.

Many Islamic scholars would argue that this approach to Islamising society is completely contrary to the spirit of Islam and the Shariah. The socio-economic realities and political dynamics in countries such as Saudi Arabia, Iran, Egypt and Pakistan mean that although the Shariah, like the rulings of the church in medieval Europe, is potentially a powerful instrument of justice, it is interpreted and applied to the advantage of wealthy and powerful men. Many Islamic scholars argue that in the modern age the principles and values of the Shariah are best realised through democratically accountable government and true rule of law. Progressive Islamic scholars generally argue that modern "western" law, properly applied, is not at odds with the Shariah but rather in fact reflects the core values of the Shariah.

Radical Islamists would take issue with their ideology being described as producing a "tyranny of a minority over a majority," preferring instead to argue that they are simply working out the will and purpose of God on earth. After all, Islam is by definition a path by which one submits to God. ("Islam" shares the same tri-consonant root – slm – as salam and its cognate, shalom, meaning peace; a M/muslim is literally one who submits to, and finds peace with, God.) What makes radical Islamism such an energetic and confronting political and social force is its certain conviction that it knows the mind of God. Its narrow epistemology, which involves a literalistic and reductionistic approach to the Qur'an and the *hadith*, and to thirteen centuries of Islamic thought, is shaped by a complex reaction to, and borrowing from, modernity. As a result, radical Islamists exchange ambiguity, ambivalence and irony for certainty, decisiveness and freedom from doubt. In embracing a worldview that sharply divides true believers from "others," they diminish their capacity for empathy, compassion and tolerance.

Radical Islamism is ultimately anti-liberal in spirit and often anti-democratic, though it is not necessarily averse to using democratic means where they offer an advantage. Nevertheless, it is important to make a distinction between radical Islamism and terrorism. Strictly speaking, terrorism is not an ideology but a means, an instrument, to achieve particular ideologically determined ends. Many who could be described as being radical Islamists on account of their ideological position would nevertheless argue earnestly and sincerely that the means of terrorism do not justify the ends of their ideology. The adoption of a radical Islamist position by no means determines that someone will support the use of violence and terrorism. This distinction is enormously important because there exists a very real danger that initiatives to root out terrorist networks will have unintended consequences, including the transformation of non-violent Islamists into militant Islamists. At the very least, harsh repression can play into the hands of Islamist terrorists by perversely boosting their personal charisma and the perceived legitimacy of their cause as they seek to seduce disillusioned youth. Already in Indonesia there is great anxiety among moderate leaders about the possibility of radicalisation as a direct consequence of what is perceived to be the indiscriminate demonising of Islam and of Muslims.

Political Islamists like Hamzah Haz seek to appeal to Islamist sentiments to win electoral support. Some hold to a deeply radical ideology and, though prepared to use democratic means, could not be said to be liberal democrats. Their long-term ambition is to bring about a radical restructuring of society (and this is where both their ideological epistemology and their strategic policy intentions become very vague) by applying the Shariah as a universal panacea, and introducing associated constitutional reform. For these radical Islamists the Iranian revolution of 1979 stands out as an inspirational example of what can be achieved by a determined minority with "God on their side" – even if they reject the revolutionary path.

Another, larger group of political Islamists is not arguing for radical change and is, in its convictions, essentially conservative. At the polling booth these candidates appeal to those for whom Islamism is an expression of conservatism. They, too, may talk of the application of the Shariah but the changes that they have in mind are modest and essentially symbolic rather than radical and profound. For these moderate political Islamists the transformation of the Indonesian state into an Islamic state along the lines of Malaysia is a much more attractive ideal than is something approaching post-revolutionary Iran. Typically, supporters of the United Development Party (PPP) would incline to moderate Islamism while supporters of the Prosperous Justice Party (PKS) and the Crescent Moon and Star Party (PBB) would incline to radical Islamism. It is not at all clear where Hamzah Haz himself stands, though he appears to align with the "right," or radical Islamist, wing of his party, PPP.

Use of the term "Islamist" has increased significantly over the past five years but a clear consensus has yet to emerge about how it should be used. Given the great cultural and social diversity found among the more than 1.3 billion Muslims living between Morocco and Indonesia, it will take time to achieve a degree of consensus on ways of describing the many subtly different political and social movements present in Muslim society. In this respect it is interesting to note that Oliver Roy, in writing about Afghanistan, draws a sharp distinction between "traditional fundamentalism" and Islamism:

> Traditional fundamentalism – that is, the will to have the Sharia and only the Sharia as the sole law – has been pervasive right through modern Afghan history... Islamism is something different: it is the perception of Islam more as a political ideology than as a mere religion. For Islamists, the Sharia is just a part of the agenda. They address society in its entirety, in politics, economics, culture and law: they claim to reshape society along purely Islamic lines. In this sense Islamism is a modern movement, the last wave of an anti-imperialist mobilization which dates back to the last century. The Islamists recruit amongst the intelligentsia and the modern strata of society, including students from "secular" faculties, mostly in sciences.

The situation in Afghanistan is, of course, strikingly different from that in Indonesia. Nevertheless Roy's description of Islamists fits well with those whom I am labelling "radical Islamists" in Indonesia, such as the cadre of PKS and PBB, and Roy's traditional fundamentalists look rather like those supporters of PPP whom I would call moderate political Islamists.

In most respects Indonesia shares much more in common with Turkey than it does with Afghanistan, or indeed any other Muslim society. So it is not surprising that in Turkey, as in Indonesia, the majority of those voting for Islamist parties appear to be social conservatives, or moderate political Islamists, rather than radical Islamists. Jenny White's observation about political Islamists in Turkey could be equally well applied to the supporters of Indonesia's PPP:

> [T]he Islamist movement in Turkey encompasses a variety of people with contradictory motivations and goals and sometimes radically differing interpretations of fundamental religious principles and political platforms. "Islam" itself takes a variety of forms. What binds people together in the Islamist movement is neither ideology (be it political or religious) nor any type of organization (whether civil society or "tribe"). Rather, the movement is rooted in local culture and interpersonal relations, while also drawing on a variety of civic and political organizations and ideologies.

Another term that is often used in discussing Indonesian Islamism is "jihadist." Using jihadist to denote militant radical Islamists is useful for distinguishing between two kinds of radical Islamists who frequently appear very similar – not least because, at times, that is their intention – despite differing in very important ways.

Jihadi Islamists, such as Abu Bakar Ba'asyir, belong in an entirely different category from radical political Islamists. They share the views of radical political Islamists but don't consider they go far enough. For them the world is divided, according to their narrow, literalistic reading of the Qur'an, between the realm of war and the realm of Islam, which is the realm of peace. Theirs is a Manichaean struggle between good and evil in which they justify pre-emptive acts of violence against those (non-Muslims or Muslims) who are said to be, collectively or individually, opposing Islam's true cause. Traditionally, jihad, which literally means "struggle," is understood in two ways. It can be regarded as a struggle to do good and especially to reform oneself, spiritually and personally; this is said to be the Greater Jihad and is much written about in the Sufi tradition. And it can be seen as an exercise in physical self-defence along the lines of just war theory – the Lesser Jihad. For jihadi Islamists, jihad is externalised and universalised as an essential component in a radical, romantically utopian, revolutionary ideology.

Contemporary jihadi Islamists tend to draw heavily on the narrowly reformist teachings of Wahhabi Islam that underlie official state Islam in Saudi Arabia. Ironically, however, they are also critical of the Saudi regime, charging it with interfering with the consistent application of Wahhabi teaching. For this reason they are sometimes described as being neo-Wahhabi because their narrow and austere understanding of Islam exceeds in strictness and zeal even the conservatism of official Saudi Wahhabism. Nevertheless, the successful promulgation of neo-Wahhabi thought around the world – often, but not always, with a jihadi Islamist emphasis – owes a great deal to the generous financial backing of powerful elements within the Saudi state.

The two-century-old sect of Islam that dominates Saudi life is referred to by outsiders as Wahhabi (or Wahabi, or Wahhabite) in recognition of the fact that it was founded by Muhammad ibn Abd al-Wahhab (c. 1703–91). Beginning in 1744, al-Wahhab, a religious scholar from the Najd region of the Arabian Peninsula's central plateau, undertook a vigorous campaign to reform Arab Islam of its many mystical and superstitious elements. Although rocky and dry, Najd is sprinkled with a myriad of little oasis communities and it was among these settlements that al-Wahhab preached his message. Ibn Abd al-Wahhab became convinced that Arab Islam had been corrupted over the previous twelve centuries by a multitude of non-Qur'anic elements. Greek philosophy was one element; ever since its first contact with, and conversion of, Byzantine Christian scholars in Syria, Islamic scholarship had been much influenced by the thought of Plato and Aristotle, culminating in the thorough-going rationalism of the Mu'tazilite school. Other elements included Sufism (Islamic mysticism much shaped by Persian and Indian thought) and folk Islam, with its emphasis on the interconnectedness of the living and the dead and especially prayer involving the mediation of dead saints. Given the strongly patriarchal nature of traditional Arab culture, it was not surprising that ibn Abd al-Wahhab was also convinced that "pure, original Islam" limited the social role of women to child-raising and housekeeping and that the Shariah's Hudud ordinances (involving stoning adulterers and amputating limbs of convicted criminals) should be interpreted absolutely literally, despite the fact that this had very rarely been the case throughout Islam's history.

In these matters ibn Abd al-Wahhab saw himself as returning Islam to the purity of the Salaf as-Salih, the Righteous Companions of the Prophet, even though many Islamic scholars would argue he completely failed to understand the dynamic flexibility and adaptiveness of early Islam, or the way in which Islam dramatically lifted the position and rights of women. Although his radical revivalist movement was out of step with mainstream Islamic thought, it did echo the narrow and aggressively doctrinaire stance of one early Islamic sect, the Kharijites. Like the Kharijites, who emerged in Islam's first century, al-Wahhab and the movement he started redefined jihad, and "the realm of war" (Dar al-Harb) in which jihad operates, to involve struggle not just with unbelievers (*kafir*) and, when forced, with "the People of the Book" (*ah'ul-kitab*) – Christians and Jews – but also with other Muslims.

Another key source of inspiration for ibn Abd al-Wahhab were the writings of the famous fourteenth-century scholar Ibn Taymiyya (1268–1323), especially those texts in which he attacked the hypocrisy of the Mongol invaders who ruled his native Iraq (forcing his family to seek refuge in Damascus) and had converted to Islam for purely instrumental reasons.

Ibn Abd al-Wahhab and the radical Islamist scholars who have come in his wake take heart from the fact that a scholar of Ibn Taymiyya's stature appears to endorse their radical position. Others, however, read Ibn Taymiyya very differently. Nurcholish Madjid, Indonesia's leading liberal Islamic intellectual, for example, wrote his doctoral dissertation on the work of Ibn Taymiyya at the University of Chicago, under the supervision of the great Pakistan-born liberal

Islamic intellectual Fazlur Rahman, and arrived at a very different understanding of Ibn Taymiyya's thought.

Unpopular with the government of his day but highly respected by his peers, Ibn Taymiyya was the greatest jurist of the Hanbali school, the narrowest of the four *mazhab*, or traditionalist schools of Sunni jurisprudence, and the school to which al-Wahhab himself belonged. Apart from his sharp critiques of religious hypocrisy, Ibn Taymiyya is famous for his call to "return to the Qur'an" and turn from complex jurisprudential reasoning (*fiqh*) to engage in direct interpretation (*ijtihad*), an emphasis that has made him popular with Islamic modernists.

Were ibn Abd al-Wahhab simply a lone reformer operating without political backing, his movement would have gone the way of the Kharijites a thousand years before it. But ibn Abd al-Wahhab did have backing: he formed a partnership with the sheikhs who ruled the Najd. They belonged to the House of Saud and their partnership with ibn Abd al-Wahhab and his followers proved remarkably resilient. For more than two centuries they enjoyed a series of advances, and endured a series of setbacks, pursuing a dream of a Saudi state that would enforce the rule of the House of Saud and "pure and true" religion in the holy cities of Mecca and Medina. Beginning in 1804 they conquered and "cleansed" the holy cities, only to be utterly vanquished by the weakened but still powerful Ottoman empire, which was deeply opposed to everything that the Saudi–Wahhabi alliance stood for: its desecration of tombs, its burning of books, its violent contempt for any expression of Islam but its own and, of course, its impertinent defiance of the ailing Ottoman empire. A bare five years later, however, the resilient regime had re-established itself in Riyadh. It was contained within the desolate interior of the peninsula for most of the nineteenth century but as the Ottoman empire entered its twilight phase at the beginning of the twentieth century, the Saudi kingdom, led by the vigorous young prince Abd al-'Aziz ibn Abd al-Rahman al-Saud, exploited tensions between the Ottoman rulers in the north and the west and British forces in the east. (The prince, commonly known as Ibn Saud, was to guide the kingdom for half a century until 1953.) By 1921 the House of Saud ruled the whole of the Najd and by 1925 it had wrested its longed-for prize of Mecca, and then Medina, from the hands of the Hashemite dynasty that had ruled the Hijaz in western Arabia and the holy cities for more than a thousand years. In 1927 Ibn Saud, ruler of the Hijaz and Najd, signed a treaty with Britain that established the basis of the modern state of Saudi Arabia.

The movement based on al-Wahhab's thinking was not popular and its survival depended on political backing. Were it not for its enduring alliance with the House of Saud the movement would have remained a purely local curiosity. And even then, were it not for three other factors it is unlikely that we would be more than remotely interested in its existence. The first of these three factors is the best understood, and concerns oil. September 1932 saw the formal declaration of the new state, the Saudi Arabian Kingdom. Six months later, on 19 May 1933, Saudi Arabia signed an agreement with Standard Oil of California, and a year later teams from Standard Oil were pumping commercial quantities of oil from the newly discovered Saudi fields and shipping them to America. Over the past 60 years the volume of oil being pumped from Saudi fields has increased dramatically from decade to decade, from 21 million barrels in 1945 to 2582 million barrels in 1975. The rest of the story is reasonably well-known: oil made the Saudi state, along with some of its neighbouring states, fantastically wealthy but that sudden wealth proved to be a very mixed blessing. Moreover, the geo-strategic importance of Saudi oil saw the House of Saud forced to prove itself simultaneously a loyal friend of America and Britain and a faithful steward and protector of Islam's holiest sites, as defined by its harshest judges, the Wahhabi clerics. The result was a monarchical state that was well aware of its vulnerability in insisting on being simultaneously both pre-modern in its religious life and pro-western in its politics. As a result, the House of Saud felt obliged to remain an uncomplainingly generous sponsor of Wahhabi proselytising around the world.

Much less well-known is the second reason why the Wahhabi movement regularly makes its presence felt in nightly news broadcasts. Wahhabism, in its eighteenth-century roots, is very much a pre-modern movement. What makes it a force in the 21st century is its cross-pollination with a very modern, very twentieth-century movement: Egypt's Muslim Brotherhood. The result is the jihadi Islamist movement that burst explosively into our awareness on 11 September

2001, having flashed repeatedly across our peripheral vision for more than a decade.

The Muslim Brotherhood was founded by Hassan al-Banna in 1928. From the outset it was a profoundly radical movement whose ultimate goal was not so much political, or even social, as spiritual in nature, as it made clear in al-Banna's "farewell" message written before his assassination in 1949:

> My Brothers, you are not a benevolent society, nor a political party, nor a local organization having political purposes. Rather you are a new soul in the heart of this nation to give it light by means of the Quran… to destroy the darkness of materialism through knowing God.

The Muslim Brotherhood under al-Banna was a modern, radical reformist movement nourished by the intellectual wellspring of Muhammad Abduh's Islamic modernism. Consequently, it too championed a "return to the Qur'an and the Sunnah," by which it meant turning to the Qur'an and the most reliable *hadith*, the sayings attributed to the Prophet, for fresh exegesis. It rejected the habit of traditionalist scholars of *taqlid*, or the acceptance of the established consensus of *ulama* in interpreting the Qur'an, arguing instead for *ijtihad*, or individual initiatives in hermeneutics producing interpretations suited to the needs of the modern age. But where Abduh was progressive and forward-looking in his approach to reform – accepting of the reality of European colonialism but determined to turn it to Islam's advantage by learning from the west – al-Banna was much more narrow. In most respects al-Banna was taking his lead from Rashid Rida, one of Abduh's most influential disciples and the man who, for many, redefined Islamic modernism after Abduh's death in 1905 through his writing in *al-Manar* (*The Lighthouse*). Unlike Abduh, Rida neither spoke a European language nor visited Europe and shared none of his master's enthusiasm for learning from the west nor his capacity to synthesise modern thought with traditional scholarship. The distinction between Abduh and Rida is very important to understanding the situation in Indonesia. Although Indonesia is home to the world's most successful modernist movement, it is also, arguably, much more influenced by Rida than by Abduh, despite common belief to the contrary.

The key figure in this drama, however, is neither al-Banna nor Rida but Sayyid Qutb. It is Qutb who built on the foundation laid by al-Banna and Rida to create one of the most complete and self-confident systems for understanding twentieth-century Islam. Qutb's abiding concern was the liberation of Muslims from *jahiliah*, the state of spiritual ignorance and depravity that caused God to send the Prophet Muhammad to Mecca thirteen centuries ago. Qutb borrowed this axial concept from the influential Pakistani Rida-oriented reformist, Abu'l Ala Maududi, whose writings had been translated into Arabic and, unusually for a non-Arab in the contemporary period, enjoyed wide acceptance. During his years in prison Qutb developed this concept to the point where he was arguing that all human society, whether in the Muslim world or in the west, was in a state of *jahiliah* so long as human authority ruled over society – in other words, unless the state was a theocracy and the only law was the Shariah. What Qutb also borrowed from Maududi was a systematic approach to articulating a modern understanding of Islam. This approach might have been simplistic in its reductionism but it was also seductively attractive in its sharp-edged eloquence. Though very much a radical Islamist, Maududi, who was also an important writer for generations of Indonesian modernists, was essentially committed to open, law-abiding, political struggle within the existing political system. His political organisation in Pakistan, Jamaat-i-Islami, though too radical ever to be truly popular, remained a regular political party and, unlike the Muslim Brotherhood, was never banned. It was Maududi who first married Lenin's idea of a radical "vanguard," a small, catalytic band of dedicated believers who would lead the revolution, with the imagery of Muhammad's early circle of Muslims who were forced to flee (*hijrah*) Mecca for Medina, an idea that Qutb picked up on.

After returning from an unpleasant but formative, or possibly confirmative, period of studying in America between 1948 and 1950, Sayyid Qutb produced a series of brilliantly earnest writings which took Maududi's radical Islamist ideas and transformed them into a powerful articulation of jihadi ideology. It was inevitable that Qutb, who took the Muslim Brotherhood, at least at the level of ideas, from local significance to global significance, would be declared an enemy of the state of Egypt and jailed for his beliefs. As with so many other radical leaders of all persuasions, his personal experience of "the struggle" confirmed and perfected his thought. His writings from inside prison attracted the intellectual interest and moral admiration of countless thousands of young Muslims across the Muslim world, not least in Indonesia, where many who had started on the "milk" of Maududi's writings graduated to the "strong meat" of Qutb.

Sayyid Qutb was elevated to the status of martyr in 1966 when he was executed in his Cairo prison. Even thorough-going progressives such as Abdurrahman Wahid, one of Indonesia's leading liberal intellectuals, were moved by Qutb's death. Abdurrahman, who had briefly indulged an interest in Qutb's writing before rejecting it as being too simplistic, stood with fellow students outside the walls of Qutb's prison keeping a vigil of prayer on the day of his execution – not, he says, because he agreed with his ideas but rather because he admired his moral courage. If Qutb's death moved a young liberal Muslim intellectual to this extent, imagine its impact on those who shared his radical convictions. Making the event even more poignant was the knowledge that Qutb had the opportunity to flee into exile but choose instead to become a martyr.

Sayyid Qutb may have gladly chosen death but he encouraged his younger brother Muhammad Qutb to join with scores of others – the cream of the Brotherhood – and flee to Saudi Arabia to continue their work. Many thousands of rank-and-file members also found lucrative employment in the buoyant Saudi economy in the 1970s and 1980s, boosting the funds available to the Brotherhood for Islamist projects across the region. The great majority of these members, and most of the Brotherhood's leadership, were not theologians like Muhammad Qutb but applied scientists and engineers, and they applied to Islam and society the same reductionistic thinking that they had learnt as technocrats. Thus it was that, beginning in the late 1960s, the pre-modern ideas of Saudi Wahhabism came to be combined with the energetic modern ideas of Sayyid Qutb. There is much more that could be told of this story but it suffices here to say that Muhammad Qutb became an influential academic in Saudi Arabia who ably communicated his elder brother's vision and ideas.

According to Paul Berman, one of his best-known students was Osama bin Laden.

The Wahhabi movement gained longevity and national significance because of its fruitful alliance with the House of Saud. It obtained international reach because of oil, as the wealthy modern Saudi state entered into a Faustian pact with Wahhabi radicalism and agreed to finance its missionary program across the globe so long as its critical energies were directed outwards to the world and not inwards to the House of Saud. The Wahhabi movement found focus, intellectual profundity and a modern revolutionary ideology when it took in sacred trust the jihadi vision of Sayyid Qutb's Muslim Brotherhood. It did not give birth to the jihadi Islamist terrorism of al-Qaeda, however, until one last critical factor was added to the cauldron. This factor was Afghanistan. When young Afghan and Pakistani *mujahidin* were joined in their struggle against the Soviets in the mid to late 1980s by fighters from Saudi Arabia and elsewhere in the Muslim world, including several thousand from Southeast Asia, jihadi Islamism entered a critical new phase. We will return to examine the details of how three factors – the radicalising experience of fighting on the battlefields of Afghanistan as *mujahidin*, the natural bonding that comes from being brothers-in-arms, and the rich experience of studying in terrorism colleges along both sides of the Afghanistan–Pakistan border as God's vanguard proven in battle – produced class after class of "Afghan alumni" ready to return home and continue the struggle.

The twentieth century is not lacking in instances of short-sighted folly in the foreign policy of western nations. High on the list of "great mistakes of our age" would have to be the decision to work with the Pakistan Inter-Services Intelligence directorate (ISI) and Saudi Arabia's foreign intelligence service, the euphemistically named Foreign Liaison Office, in sponsoring *mujahidin* to fight against the Soviets in Afghanistan. Of course, in the late 1980s it was no more expected that the Cold War would be followed by the War on Terrorism involving these very *mujahidin* than it was that the Berlin Wall would fall overnight in a sudden peaceful uprising. And so it was that expediency which sought to speed the denouement of one century's bad dream helped to beget the next century's nightmare.

Although it has now become common to talk of the alarming spread of Wahhabism around the world, in belated recognition of Saudi Arabia's dangerous but previously ignored export trade in extremism and hatred, jihadi Islamists generally don't describe themselves as being Wahhabi or neo-Wahhabi. Instead they use the term Salafy, which invokes the (imagined) "pure Islam" of the first century of Islam, as practised by the Prophet and his companions. The problem with this terminology is that a great many Islamic groups and institutions are described as being Salafy; for many this term simply denotes a commitment to Islamic reform, and it is often used by Islamic modernists to describe their more "rational" and "scripturally based" interpretation of Islam compared to Islamic traditionalists.

Given al-Wahhab's radical objection to the veneration of saints it is hardly surprising that those who closely follow his teachings do not wish to be known by his name. They generally refer to themselves simply as Muwahhidin – the people of *tawhid*, or the Unity of God.

Further confusing the matter is the fact that jihadi Islamists often describe themselves as being followers of "al sunnah wal jamaah." This term simply means "of the Way [of The Prophet Muhammad] and of the Community [of Muslims]." But like Salafy – even more so – "al sunnah wal jamaah" is used to denote Sunni (as opposed to Shia) Islamic traditionalism. Nahdlatul Ulama (NU) members typically use it to describe their kind of traditional, folk Islam, richly imbued with various strains of Sufi mysticism of differing degrees of orthodoxy and syncretistic appropriation of pre-Islamic religion. Yet the term is also used by radical Islamists; the organisation behind Laskar Jihad, for example, describes itself as Forum Komunikasi Ahlus Sunnah wal Jamaah (the Communications Forum of the People of the Sunnah wal Jamaah), and there are a number of jihadi groups around the world that use similar names. To the neo-Wahhabi, Salafy, jihadi Islamists of al-Qaeda and Jemaah Islamiyah, NU's kind of Islam is a complete anathema, for they reject every suggestion of folk Islam superstition and mysticism.

It also needs to be noted that for several decades in Indonesia and Malaysia many individuals and groups influenced by Wahhabism have remained essentially quiescent in their expression of Islam. That is to say, they, like the Amish, have been "fundamentalists" in their narrow, scripturalist interpretation of religion but their activism has focused on personal spiritual development rather than radical politics, and as individuals and communities they have turned inward in their attempts to find a sanctified space for piety and have not attempted to recreate the state in their image. Martin van Bruinessen argues that:

> Most of the student groups were quietist and apolitical; they were primarily concerned with individual moral self-improvement and with the *Usroh* as a moral haven in an immoral world. But there were also *Usroh* groups affiliated with such NII/TII leaders as Abu Bakar Ba'asyir, which believed in the necessity of establishing an Islamic state and imposing the Sharia on fellow Muslims. No firm boundaries between these various groups existed.

A vitally important area to watch in Indonesia in the coming years is the synergistic relationship between jihadi and political Islamism and the degree to which jihadi Islamism exerts influence over, and is supported by, political Islamism. Also important to watch is the transformation of previously quiescent Islamic fundamentalists into active Islamist radicals no longer merely content to cast their vote for the Islamist parties but rather feeling compelled to enter into the struggle to change society directly.

CHAPTER 3
Jemaah Islamiyah's struggle

The al-Qaeda attacks on America on 11 September 2001 caused western observers to begin to see Southeast Asian Islam afresh and conferred on the region's small bands of radical Islamists a prominence that, prior to the Bali bombing at least, seemed out of all proportion with their limited domestic appeal. After September 11 a quiet debate developed among observers. While some pointed to links between militant Islamism in the "Malay" world of archipelago Southeast Asia and extremist movements in the Arab world and South and West Asia, others questioned the evidence for such links and used demography to downplay the importance of radical groups. In Indonesia especially, observers were divided on how to assess the threat of Islamist radicalism and on how to respond to it.

Some saw the unfettered existence of vigilante groups such as Laskar Jihad, apparently supported by elements within the military elite, and the involvement of such militias in fatal violence in Maluku and Central Sulawesi, as deeply troubling developments. At the very least, they argued, Indonesia's current chronic state of disarray and the dysfunctional nature of much of the state apparatus, especially outside Java, left it dangerously vulnerable to international radical Islamist networks operating within the archipelago. Other observers, however, argued that the threat of radical Islamism in Indonesia was greatly overstated and that little hard evidence existed that international radical elements and terrorist networks were involved in local affairs. Virtually all observers agreed that the vast majority of Indonesian Muslims are personally tolerant and moderate in their outlook and are generally opposed to militant radicalism.

What, then, are we to make of concerns about radical Islamism in Indonesia? Certainly, the moderate nature of Indonesia's two mass-based Islamic organisations, the 40-million-strong Nahdlatul Ulama (NU) and the 30-million-strong Muhammadiyah is widely seen as underwriting the essentially quiescent and tolerant nature of Indonesian Islam. Together the two organisations represent a major portion of all Indonesian Muslims, and the great majority of all *santri* Muslims, the observant Muslims who pray and fast regularly and observe orthodox practices. Many see this as reason for believing that radical Islamism will never be more than a peripheral phenomenon in Indonesia. Further supporting a sanguine reading of Islamic politics and social movements in Indonesia is the fact that traditional Islam in Indonesia is highly Sufistic and richly imbued with the tolerant syncretism of folk Islam.

At the same time, totally denying the influence of globalised radical Islamism in Southeast Asian society would be almost as foolish as succumbing to essentialism. Radical Islamism might only enjoy a very limited following in Indonesia but that does not mean that we should not give it serious attention. Indeed, the evidence that has come to light in the wake of the Bali bombing means that we no longer have the luxury of telling ourselves that we should not be overly worried about militant Islamism in Indonesia because "Indonesia is different." In the months since the bombing, a disturbing picture has emerged of a highly radicalised militant movement that, while still very small in absolute terms, is more deeply rooted in Indonesian society and more extensively integrated into international terrorist networks than we had previously recognised. Indonesia is different, but not so different that it remains untouched by the same globalising forces of radicalism that have taken root in other parts of the Muslim world.

Since the fall of Soeharto in May 1998, radical Islamism has been centre stage to an extent that is entirely out of proportion to its size, and in the run-up to general elections in April 2004 it enjoyed considerable immunity from public censure. Why? First, Islamism has arguably always had stronger support in Indonesia than is generally acknowledged. In his final decade in power, Soeharto himself recognised this and actively courted Islamist support, in the process allowing the Islamist radicals he had previously persecuted to "come in from the cold" and entrench themselves within the establishment.

Ironically, Soeharto's action contributed to the growth of support for radical Islamism within the senior ranks of the military. The economic crisis of 1997 broke like a storm over Soeharto's already weakened regime and, as it began to disintegrate, radical Islamist militias linked to factions within the military began to incite and exacerbate inter-communal tensions in a society stressed by economic collapse.

The tragic consequences of their activities were all too apparent during the brief reformist presidency of liberal Islamic intellectual, and long-time leader of NU, Abdurrahman Wahid, when thousands died in inter-communal conflict in Ambon and its hinterland, and in North Maluku and Central Sulawesi. Wahid provoked the ire of the Islamists with his progressive policies. They quickly came to regret their part in his election and led the push to replace this independently minded reformer with the quiescent Megawati Sukarnoputri.

As was noted in chapter 1, the first exhaustive review of reliable, public data about Jemaah Islamiyah links in Indonesia prior to the Bali bombing investigations was a report published by the International Crisis Group (ICG) in August 2002. It focused on the loose network of radical Islamists associated with the Pondok Ngruki *pesantren*, led by the outspoken preacher Abu Bakar Ba'asyir and situated in the village of Ngruki near Solo in Central Java. The word *pesantren* is Javanese in origin and describes the sort of religious boarding school that elsewhere in the Muslim world would be known as *madrasah*. (Confusingly, the term *madrasah* is also used of thousands of religious schools in Indonesia, though generally in Indonesia these are day schools and have a largely secular curriculum. Most *pesantren* also house *madrasah* within their complexes. *Pesantren* tend to be associated with NU, and non-*pesantren*-linked *madrasah* with the modernist Islamist organisation Muhammadiyah, but there are many *pesantren* that are independent of both organisations.) Abu Bakar Ba'asyir – who is also Commander of the Majelis Mujahidin Indonesia (MMI – the Indonesian Mujahidin Council), the radical organisation founded in Yogyakarta in 2000, to which many Pondok Ngruki graduates belong – draws inspiration from the Darul Islam (abode of Islam) rebellion led by Sekarmadji Maridjan Kartosuwirjo in West Java in the 1950s.

Active in the nationalist movement before the second world war, Kartosuwirjo was one of the principal organisers of Hizbullah, a militia set up during Japanese occupation by the peak Islamic organisation Masyumi and later marshalled to fight the Dutch. Although Kartosuwirjo played a significant role in Masyumi's post-war transformation into a political party, he grew increasingly unhappy with the moderate direction it took. In January 1948, refusing to go along with an agreement between the other nationalists and the Dutch that would have required revolutionary forces to withdraw from parts of Java, Kartosuwirjo established the Tentara Islam Indonesia (TII – Islamic Army of Indonesia) in West Java. A year and a half later, on 7 August 1949, he proclaimed the creation of Negara Islam Indonesia (NII – Islamic State of Indonesia) and declared the districts controlled by his troops to be Darul Islam, a move which brought him into direct conflict with the nationalist forces. Kartosuwirjo's forces engaged in periodic skirmishes with the Indonesian military (TNI – Tentara Nasional Indonesia) up until 1962, when Kartosuwirjo was finally arrested.

In South Sulawesi another former Hizbullah leader and respected nationalist, Kahar Muzakkar, upset with the refusal of TNI officers to grant places within TNI to members of his militia, refused orders to demobilise his men and instead declared that they would fight for the rights of the people of Sulawesi. In 1952 he made contact with Kartosuwirjo and the next year, inspired by the success of Kartosuwirjo's Darul Islam in West Java, he proclaimed that Sulawesi was part of the Negara Republik Islam Indonesia (NRII – Islamic Republic of Indonesia). Kahar Muzakkar's rebellion, which began as a regional-rights dispute and only later became radicalised along Islamist lines, continued until his death at the hands of the TNI in 1965.

After the collapse of the West Java and South Sulawesi rebellions, relatively little was heard about Darul Islam–style radical Islamism in Indonesia until the late 1970s. In mid-1977 the Soeharto regime arrested 185 people, many with Darul Islam connections, whom it accused of belonging to an organisation it referred to as Komando Jihad. It is not clear whether this fresh crackdown on radical Islamism was precipitated by a genuine, grassroots resurgence of interest in Darul Islam radicalism or whether the Indonesian military (known at this time as ABRI – Angkatan Bersenjata Republik Indonesia, the Indonesian Armed Forces) was simply attempting to flush out, and make an example of, radical Islamists ahead of the 1977 general elections. What has long been suspected, and what the ICG was able to verify, was that General Ali Murtopo, Soeharto's notorious "Special Operations" manager, and his officers within BAKIN, the ABRI intelligence agency, engaged in an elaborate sting operation that lured hundreds of former Darul Islam fighters out of hiding. Selling the line that the fall of Saigon in 1975 heralded the danger of communist advances throughout Southeast Asia and formed a challenge that required the forces of the right to work together – and possibly also offering financial inducements – Murtopo's men were able to persuade key former Darul Islam members to contact their colleagues and reactivate their movement. This resulted in the establishment of Jemaah Islamiyah (the term, which was to be commonly invoked by the Indonesian military in subsequent decades, is very non-specific and simply means community/ies of Islam) as a precursor to a new Darul Islam movement. While Murtopo appeared to have nothing more extensive in mind than a sting operation (there being no suggestion that Murtopo's group contained anyone with Islamist sympathies, or that he was seeking to co-opt Islamist activists to use against rivals within the regime), its impact is still being felt. As the August 2002 ICG report on the Ngruki network observed:

> The operation set in motion by Ali Moertopo and the Indonesian intelligence in the 1970s had several unintended consequences. It renewed or forged bonds amongst Muslim radicals in South Sulawesi, Sumatra, and Java. It promoted the idea of an Islamic state in a way that the original Darul Islam leaders had perhaps not intended, and in doing so tapped an intellectual ferment that was particularly pronounced in university-based mosques. That ferment was only beginning when Komando Jihad was created, but through the late 1970s and early 1980s, it was fuelled by the Iranian revolution, the availability of Indonesian translations of writings on political Islam from the Middle East and Pakistan; and anger over Soeharto government policies.

Together with Abu Bakar Ba'asyir, the other key leader of the so-called Komando Jihad–Jemaah Islamiyah identified by Indonesian intelligence was Abdullah Sungkar from Brebes, Central Java, who was arrested in November 1978. Like Ba'asyir, Sungkar, a former officer in Kartosuwirjo's TII, was born in Java in the late 1930s of Yemeni descent. Both men had long careers as Islamic activists beginning with years spent in the Masyumi-affiliated Indonesian Muslim Youth Movement, followed by periods of missionary activism that saw Ba'asyir join al-Irsyad (an Islamist organisation supported particularly by Indonesian Muslims of Arab descent) and Sungkar join Masyumi. The two men first began to work together in 1967 when they founded first Radio Dakwah Islamiyah Surakata in Solo in 1967, and then Pesantren al-Mukmin (later better known as Pondok Ngruki) in 1971.

Abu Bakar Ba'asyir and Abdullah Sungkar were finally tried in 1982 and both were initially sentenced to nine years in prison; these sentences were overturned on appeal, however, and the pair were released with their sentences being reduced to the three years and ten months they had served prior to their trial. Returning to Pondok Ngruki they worked hard to build up a network of supporters. If the alleged Jemaah Islamiyah network of the 1970s was substantially a fiction created by BAKIN, during the mid-1980s it was made a reality by Ba'asyir and Sungkar and their followers, newly radicalised by the experience of military repression. Ba'asyir and Sungkar encouraged their followers to return to their villages and establish cells of around a dozen members, to live communally and to avoid all non-Islamic institutions. As well as in Solo, Islamist discussion groups and cells emerged in nearby Yogyakarta. In this city of universities and colleges many students who were angry with the increasingly corrupt and repressive Soeharto regime, and disillusioned with the west that supported it, found inspiration in the 1979 Islamic revolution in Iran. They translated and published, and read and discussed, the writings of Islamist intellectuals such as Ali Shariati and Murtaza Mutahhari of Iran, Hassan al-Banna and Sayyid Qutb of Egypt's Muslim Brotherhood, and Abu'l Ala Maududi of Pakistan's Jamaat-i-Islami. Martin van Bruinessen observes:

> It was the ban of Masyumi and the general depoliticisation imposed on Indonesian Islam under Suharto that caused a turn to Islamic

thought. The ideas of the Muslim Brotherhood then became a major focus of orientation for people of Masyumi background. Initially the Islamic socialism of the Syrian Brother Mustafa al-Siba'i (whose book *Islamic Socialism* was translated early, banned under Suharto, and later reprinted with a different title) had a strong appeal, reflecting Masyumi's social democratic leaning. Later al-Banna became the leading authority, along with the Pakistani Abu'l-A'la Mawdudi. Several of Sayyid Qutb's were also translated, including *Ma'alim fi'l-tariq* (*Signposts on the Road*), but his more radical political ideas appear not to have made the impact in Indonesia that they made elsewhere. It was the non-revolutionary, Saudi-sponsored brand of Brotherhood materials that became most influential in former Masyumi circles in the 1980s and 1990s.

Adding to the radicalisation of the young men drawn to Ngruki was the bitter experience of the September 1984 riots in Jakarta's port district of Tandjung Priok. The Tandjung Priok incident, in which – conservatively estimated – dozens of members of local mosque communities and *usrah* activist cells were shot dead by troops under the command of General Benny Murdani, a Catholic, was clearly intended to intimidate the Islamists. This it did, but it also radicalised many more and hardened their resolve to work for change.

In February 1985 a prosecution appeal was lodged with the Supreme Court challenging the reduced sentences awarded to Ba'asyir and Sungkar. Faced with the possibility of a further period of detention the pair decided to flee to Malaysia. In the wake of their flight, and following the arrest of a former Pondok Ngruki lecturer, Abdul Qadir Baraja, over the January 1985 bombing of the Buddhist stupa of Borobudur outside Yogyakarta, the *usrah*–Jemaah Islamiyah network in Central Java began to break up, or at least go to ground.

On his way to Malaysia in 1985 Abdullah Sungkar stopped briefly in Lampung, South Sumatra, an area that was home to tens of thousands of trans-migrants from Central and East Java. He quickly developed a local following that coalesced around an Islamiyah community (*jemaah*) in the village of Talangsari in the district of Way Jepara, Lampung province. In time the community attracted members fleeing persecution in Central and East Java; some of the newcomers had links with the earlier Darul Islam movements in West Java and Aceh and with Abdul Qadir Baraja, who was by this time serving a fifteen-year jail sentence. By 1989 the group, which was increasingly known for its hard-line views, had attracted adverse attention from the local authorities. Warsidi, the man who had donated the land on which the community was established, was summoned to appear before the local military commander. When he refused, nine of his followers were taken into custody. Fearing imminent attack the community armed itself and prepared for confrontation. The tense stand-off came to a violent end when the sub-district military commander was hacked to death when he went to speak with Warsidi. Predictably, the killing met with an overwhelming response from the military. The following day, when most of the men had gone into hiding in the surrounding jungle, the compound was overrun by the military. Led by the head of the local military command, Colonel Hendropriyono, the reprisal is widely regarded as a massive overreaction, though probably one that was carefully calculated to send a strong message to other hard-line communities. It is thought that at least 100 people, many of whom were women and children, were killed. Today Lt Gen. Hendropriyono is head of Badan Intelijens Nasional (BIN), the national intelligence agency, and is a key figure in President Megawati's cabinet.

While in self-imposed exile in Malaysia, Ba'asyir and Sungkar continued to maintain links with associates in Indonesia, not just in Central Java but also in Jakarta, in West Java, North Sumatra and South Sulawesi, where they were able to recruit small numbers of volunteer *mujahidin* fighters for the struggle against the Soviets in Afghanistan. In the mid-1990s Ba'asyir and Sungkar significantly shifted their position following contact with Usama Rushdi of Gama Islami, the radical breakaway faction of Egypt's Muslim Brotherhood. Gama Islami (or al-Gama'at al-Islamiyah, to give it its full name) is closely linked to al-Qaeda and was led by Sheikh Umar Abdul Rahman, the Islamist teacher convicted in the United States for his part in the 1993 World Trade Center bombing. The Gama Islami connection saw Ba'asyir and Sungkar move beyond the old Darul Islam vision of establishing an Islamic state within Indonesia, or at least making the Indonesian state more Islamic, to the more radical, pan-Islam position calling for the re-establishment of an international Islamic caliphate. Although this shift initially caused some dispute within the Ngruki exile community, it came to be accepted by the network as a whole.

Following President Soeharto's resignation in May 1998, Ba'asyir and Sungkar returned to Java. Sungkar died soon after but Abu Bakar Ba'asyir was able to re-establish himself in Pondok Ngruki from where he spearheaded a push to unite all groups wishing to implement the Shariah in Indonesia. In August 2000, at a time when President Abdurrahman Wahid was facing overt challenges from radical Islamist groups (including the Laskar Jihad militia, which had been established earlier that year and had sent thousands of fighters to Maluku despite the president's orders), Ba'asyir was able to organise a three-day Mujahidin Congress in Yogyakarta. This remarkable gathering drew delegates from across the archipelago representing virtually every Islamist group in the country. The main achievement of the congress, apart from its success as a show of strength, was the establishment of the Majelis Mujahidin Indonesia (MMI – Indonesian Mujahidin Council), dedicated to preparing the way for the establishment of a new international caliphate. Significantly, Hizb ut-Tahrir, the Jordan-based militant Islamist organisation calling for the re-establishment of the caliphate, sent a number of observers to the congress in Yogyakarta, an indication of its growing influence in Indonesia. (Interestingly, the Indonesian branch of Hizb ut-Tahrir was established by visiting Australian members of the organisation.) Abu Bakar Ba'asyir was declared Amir ul-Mujahidin, or commander, of MMI's governing council and Abdul Qadir Baraja was appointed head of its fatwa section. Other people closely linked with the Ngruki network, including a number who had fought in Afghanistan and studied in Pakistan, made up much of the leadership of MMI.

The four main Indonesians first recognised as having close links with al-Qaeda are all connected to Pondok Ngruki. The first is Fathur Rahman al-Ghozi, who was arrested in Manila in January 2002 on suspicion of involvement in a series of bombings in Manila in December 2000 and a planned attack in Singapore. He was alleged in court to have had illegal explosives and false documents in his possession when arrested, and to have subsequently confessed to being involved in the Manila bombings; on the strength of this evidence he was sentenced to eighteen years in jail. On 14 July 2003, al-Ghozi escaped from "tight security" when he simply walked out of his Manila jail, leaving behind serious questions about the integrity and competence of the Philippines police force. He was later shot dead when police closed in on him in his Mindanao hideout and so is no longer available for questioning. The second is Hambali, said to be al-Qaeda's main contact in Indonesia and allegedly linked with bombings in Jakarta and Manila in December 2000 and a planned attack on American navy personnel in Singapore. The third is Abu Jibril, currently under detention in Malaysia. He is said to be al-Qaeda's main financial courier in Southeast Asia and appears in a videotape recruiting fighters for Maluku. And the fourth is Agus Dwikarna, who has been under detention in the Philippines since his arrest in March 2002. Although it is alleged that he was apprehended carrying a suitcase containing explosives, there are credible counter-claims that these were planted. He too is said to be involved with the Jakarta and Manila bombings.

The ICG report concluded by sagely considering the question of "what to do now":

> Association with the Ngruki network is not equivalent to terrorism, and yet the possibility remains that some members of the exile group who have since returned to Indonesia may be sources of support for criminal activities. But repression helped give birth to the network, and it would be a major mistake to encourage the Indonesian government, or other governments in the region, to re-institute the kind of arbitrary practices that Soeharto's resignation was supposed to bring to an end.

The 200 JI operatives arrested as a result of the Polri–AFP breakthrough after the Bali bombing have yielded a wealth of information about how JI operates and what it has been doing. It soon emerged that JI cells were behind the Christmas Eve bombings in Medan, on the east coast of Sumatra, in Pekanbaru, capital of the nearby province of Riau, and in the West Java cities of Bandung, Sukabumi and Ciamis. It also emerged that Hambali, the mastermind of the Bali bombing, planned the West Java Christmas Eve bombings and recruited foot soldiers for such operations. Testimony from JI detainees also confirmed much of the content of the September 2003 *Time* magazine report about Omar al-Faruq and JI's al-Qaeda connections. From their confessions a picture has emerged about the training of JI operatives in Pakistan and Mindanao, with details that could only be guessed at prior to the Bali bombing. Based on this data, the August 2003 ICG report draws the conclusion that:

> If some early accounts painted JI as an al-Qaeda affiliate, tightly integrated with the bin Laden network, the reality is more complex. JI has elements in common with al-Qaeda, particularly its jihadist ideology and a long period of shared experience in Afghanistan. Its leaders revere bin Laden and seek to emulate him, and they have almost certainly received direct financial support from al-Qaeda. But JI is not operating simply as an al-Qaeda subordinate. Virtually all of its decision-making and much of its fund-raising has been conducted locally, and its focus, for all the claims about its wanting to establish a South East Asia caliphate, continues to be on establishing an Islamic state in Indonesia...
>
> JI also maintains alliance with a loose network of like-minded regional organizations all committed in different ways to jihad. The Makassar bombings of 5 December 2002 were not the work of JI, for example, but they were carried out by men who had been trained by JI in Mindanao and who had the motivation, manpower, and skills to undertake a JI-like attack. JI had also made very pragmatic use of thugs (*preman*) as necessary, particularly in Ambon.

It is now clear that the members of JI's senior leadership fought and trained in Afghanistan and Pakistan between 1985 and 1995, as did many of its key operatives, including those later involved in carrying out bomb attacks in Indonesia and the Philippines. For these JI leaders the experience in Afghanistan and Pakistan was clearly formative and radicalising. For some younger members, fighting as *mujahidin* in Maluku and Sulawesi and training in Mindanao appear to have proved similarly formative and radicalising. Even now it is not at all clear how many Indonesians went to Afghanistan and Pakistan although it is possible that many hundreds were involved.

The first small (possibly less than a dozen-strong) cohort of Indonesian *mujahidin* were sent to Pakistan by Abdullah Sungkar in 1985 at around the time that Sungkar and Ba'asyir were forced to flee Indonesia for Malaysia and when fighting against the Soviets in Afghanistan entered its bloodiest phase. They were followed in 1986 by a much larger group of around 50 or 60 recruits.

The early Southeast Asian recruits were sent first to Peshawar, Pakistan, where they were systematically processed by a *maktab*, or college (Maktab al-Khidmat), established in 1984. This *maktab* was under the command of Abdullah Azzam, a charismatic Jordanian–Palestinian much admired by Osama bin Laden and later a key al-Qaeda ideologue whose writing was translated and published in Indonesian by members of Ba'asyir's *pesantren* in Ngruki. The recruits were then sent to Camp Saddah, the camp in Khumran Agency, at Parachinar in Pakistan, run by Abdul Rasul Sayyaf, an Afghan *mujahidin* commander and Saudi-backed, strict neo-Wahhabi with close ties to Osama bin Laden.

Many of these early Indonesian *mujahidin*, including those who later became key JI leaders, experienced a baptism by fire when they fought alongside bin Laden and other future al-Qaeda leaders in the famous, weeks-long Battle of Jaji in which the underdog *mujahidin* guerrillas succeeded in stopping a Soviet advance.

When the second cohort of Indonesian recruits arrived in 1986, Sayyaf offered to help them establish a discrete training camp within the Camp Saddah complex, providing them not only with the land but also with food and firearms. Camp Saddah was divided into a series of *qabilah*, or tribes, and the Southeast Asian recruits were collectively regarded as forming one tribe. The camp also housed a Central Arab (Egypt, Jordan, Saudi) tribe and a Maghrib (Algeria, Tunisia) tribe, with each group tending to stick to themselves.

Key JI operatives such as Fathur Rahman al-Ghozi (a graduate of Ba'asyir's *pesantren* in Ngruki) and Imam Samudra (later sentenced to death for his part in masterminding the Bali bombing) trained in Camp Saddah. Beginning in 1991, recruits from Indonesia, Malaysia and Singapore commenced a formal three-year course of training in the camp.

In 1992 Abdullah Sungkar and Ajengan Masduki, who worked closely together as leaders of those identified with Darul Islam in Indonesia, had a severe personal falling out, with the former accusing the latter of Shia and Sufi tendencies (which were heavily criticised in neo-Wahhabi circles). In the wash-up Sungkar travelled to Camp Saddah and, after outlining his case, asked the recruits to choose between him and Masduki. According to the ICG report, the rift "resulted directly in JI's creation as an organisation separate and distinct from Darul Islam."

After a *mujahidin* coalition government in Afghanistan was established in 1992, JI moved from Camp Saddah and established a new camp outside Torkham, Afghanistan. Fathur Rahman al-Ghozi became a prominent leader there and it was at the camp that he befriended Moro Islamic Liberation Front leaders from the Philippines – including two men, Salahudin and Habib, who were to work with him years later on the Rizal Day bombing in Manila. This friendship became significant when the JI leadership later asked al-Ghozi to establish a JI training facility within Camp Abu Bakar in Mindanao.

The August 2003 ICG report details seven distinct "classes" or cohorts of students at Camp Saddah, who undertook a three-year course of training (though many opted for shorter periods) between 1985 and 1991. Beginning in 1991 recruits headed directly to Afghanistan, with many training in the new camp outside Torkham.

In 1996 JI training shifted to its own Camp Hudaibiyah in a remote corner of the sprawling Camp Abu Bakar complex in Mindanao. It appears that several hundred Indonesians trained at this new JI camp. Camp Hudaibiyah was divided into its own "tribes," in this case encompassing Camp Solo, Camp Banten and Camp Sulawesi, for recruits from Javanese Central Java, Sundanese West Java and Sulawesi respectively. Camp Abu Bakar was overrun by the Philippines military in 2000. Although this setback did not see the end of JI training in the Philippines, it did prompt JI to set up a new training camp in Poso, Central Sulawesi.

At around the same time, Abdullah Sungkar and other senior "Afghan alumni" formalised the structure of JI and set it forth in a small book entitled *General Guidelines for the Jemaah Islamiyah Struggle*. According to the book, the command structure for JI was topped by an *amir* – Abdullah Sungkar (and, after he died in 1999, Abu Bakar Ba'asyir) – who appointed and directed a governing council. The council was headed by central command overseeing four *mantiqi*, or geographical spheres of operation (Mantiqi I: Malaysia–Singapore; Mantiqi II: Western Indonesia; Mantiqi III: Mindanao, Sabah and Sulawesi; and Mantiqi IV: Papua and Australia).

According to the ICG, "it is probably more appropriate to think of JI as a military structure, befitting a guerrilla army, with brigades (*mantiqi*); battalions (*wakalah*); companies (*khatibah*); platoons (*qirdas*); and squads (*fiah*)." It appears that JI also has one or more Laskar Khos, or special operations unit/s, which may have been responsible for the Marriott Hotel bombing in Jakarta.

Even though JI has its own well-defined command structure, it is clear that the organisation actively encourages cooperation with other like-minded jihadi Islamist groups in complex ways. Some JI operatives, for example, assisted the South Sulawesi groups Wahdah Islamiyah and Laskar Jundullah to carry out the Makassar bombings on 5 December 2002, killing three people in a McDonald's restaurant and wrecking a car dealership showroom belonging to the Coordinating Minister for People's Welfare, Yusuf Kalla. Kalla was unpopular among radical Islamists because he brokered a peace deal between Christians and Muslims in Poso, Central Sulawesi.

Although the senior leadership of JI are all "Afghan alumni," many of its foot soldiers are simple *pesantren* graduates. It needs to be stressed, however, that the vast majority of Indonesia's 25,000 *pesantren* teach a moderate rather than radical understanding of Islam. There are only five *pesantren* known to be closely linked to JI and teaching a jihadi interpretation of Islam: Pesantren al-Mukmin in Ngruki; Pesantren Sukohardjo in Solo; Pesantren Al-Muttaqien in Jepara, Central Java; Pesantren Dar us-Syahadah in Boyolali, Central Java; and Pesantren al-Islam in Lamongan, East Java. To this list could also be added Lukmanul Hakiem, in Johor, Malaysia, but this *pesantren* was closed by the Malaysian authorities in 2001. Outside this small "Ivy League" group of *pesantren* the ICG report identifies a larger group of jihadi *pesantren* located in Java, Kalimantan and Sulawesi. Fortunately, unlike the situation in Pakistan where a much larger proportion of *madrasah* actively support jihadi extremism, these *pesantren* are but a small fraction of all *pesantren* in Indonesia.

Clearly, the alumni network of *pesantren* graduates is an important element within the JI structure. But also of great importance are the bonds formed through marriage alliances across Southeast Asia, particularly between Malaysian and Indonesian members of JI.

What initially appeared to be a serious but relatively limited terrorist threat when the Bali bombing investigations began in October 2002 was steadily revealed to be a disturbingly well-established network with at least 300–400, and possibly many more, operatives. And any thought that the threat from JI was finally under control was rudely confronted on 5 August 2003 when a suicide bomber detonated his explosive-laden Toyota Kijang on the driveway ramp of Jakarta's prestigious JW Marriott Hotel, killing twelve people and injuring more than 150. Had security guards not stopped the bomber at the base of the ramp, possibly preventing him from crashing through the Marriott's glass doors and detonating inside the foyer, the death toll may have been very much higher. In August 2003, following the public announcement of Hambali's capture, US Deputy Secretary of State Richard Armitage observed (in what may be an overstatement but was based on good intelligence and military experience): "The difference between the 12 unfortunate souls who lost their lives in Jakarta and literally hundreds losing their life, was about four feet of distance from where the car was parked."

Hambali's capture is the single most important achievement in a series of significant breakthroughs but it is clear that a long and difficult struggle lies ahead before the threat of radical Islamist terrorism can finally be said to be under control.

At the same time, the "half pregnant" verdict in the 2003 trial of Abu Bakar Ba'asyir undid much of the good work done in building public support for moving against JI, with even moderate Islamic leaders beginning to openly question the strength of the real evidence against Ba'asyir and JI.

Few accept in totality the bizarre conspiracy theories promulgated by a number of public figures, including convicted Bali bomber Amrozi and Abu Bakar Ba'asyir himself, but there is a worrying degree of acceptance of more modest speculation about possible conspiracies, particularly those involving either the Indonesian military or, as Ba'asyir has argued, some dark alliance of western agencies including "the CIA and the Jews." Furthermore, while the rapid military defeat of the regime of Saddam Hussein in Iraq dissipated the mounting waves of protest against the war that had begun to unite Islamic moderates and radicals, the war and its messy aftermath have left a residue of antipathy towards the United States and its "imperialist" allies across the region.

In this context, it is a great pity, to say the least, that the prosecution case against Ba'asyir was not handled more competently. Admittedly the presence in court of Kuwaiti al-Qaeda operative Omar al-Faruq and JI's own Hambali, both currently in American detention, would have greatly strengthened the case against Ba'asyir, but even without them there was a large volume of evidence that could have been tendered in court but was not. It is rather surprising, for example, that detained JI operative Mohammed Nasir bin Abbas was not called to testify. In late July he had appeared in court in Denpasar to deliver damning evidence against JI, Ba'asyir and the alleged Bali bombers, describing how he and Mukhlas (who later married his sister) met with Ba'asyir in Malaysia in 1987 and were sent by him to fight as *mujahidin* in Afghanistan and then to undertake a three-year course of studies at Camp Saddah.

Nasir bin Abbas went on to explain that after he and Mukhlas returned to Malaysia they lived with Ba'asyir. At the time the Southeast Asian *mujahidin* referred to their group as Darul Islam, deliberately evoking memories of the Darul Islam rebellion in West Java in the 1950s. He said that in 1993, however, Sungkar and Ba'asyir announced that they would be known as Jemaah Islamiyah and that a new structure had begun to take shape. For reasons that are not clear, Nasir bin Abbas was not summoned as a witness in the Ba'asyir trial and in the end only one witness, Faiz Abu Bakar Bafana, provided useful and extensive testimony. Although Bafana's testimony was also very damning of Ba'asyir, it was largely discounted by the judges, partly because Bafana, a Malaysian national detained in Singapore, gave evidence only via videolink and the prosecution had failed to arrange for him to be cross-examined, and partly because his testimony was at variance with that of the other witnesses. For this reason the judges found Ba'asyir guilty of involvement with JI but said that insufficient proof was submitted that he had become the *amir*, or spiritual leader, of JI following Sungkar's death in 1999. He was sentenced to just four years in jail, one of which he had already served.

The ramifications of the Ba'asyir trial threaten to be far-reaching, not so much because Ba'asyir was an important leader in JI (in operational terms Hambali was far more important), but because Ba'asyir was cleverly manipulating public opinion to undermine the government's assertion that JI exists and that it is responsible for the Marriott and Bali bombings. By making the counter-assertion that there is no such organisation as JI and that the bombings where a CIA ploy to discredit Islam, Ba'asyir sowed seeds of doubt in the fertile imaginations of an Indonesian public still reeling from the judgement of the international community that their tolerant and generous society had given birth to al-Qaeda-style terrorism. That lies as audacious as Ba'asyir's should have any currency at all is an indication of just how troubled the psyche of Indonesian society continues to be after five years of crisis and bad press. But backed by the authority of the judge's verdict, Ba'asyir's mendacious refrain worked its spell even on some of the most moderate of Islamic leaders.

Nahdlatul Ulama chairman Hasyim Muzadi recently claimed that the United States was talking up the threat of JI in order to have its way with the governments of Indonesia and its Muslim neighbours. One day after the United States had frozen the assets and bank accounts of ten suspected JI terrorists, most of whom were Indonesian, Muzadi invoked the judge's findings, saying, "The verdict is proof that JI does not exist in Indonesia, even if it exists in other countries." He went on to argue, "Islam is not radical and does not subscribe to terrorism. Radicalism may happen, but it is only a reaction to injustice that the US itself has perpetrated, for example, in the case of Palestine." Echoing Muzadi's scepticism, Ahmad Syafi'i Ma'arif, chairman of Muhammadiyah and one of Indonesia's leading progressive Islamic intellectuals, recently observed that if Ba'asyir "is only guilty by association, then the old man should be freed."

Scepticism in the wake of a bungled prosecution case is one thing but it is quite another for moderate, mainstream Islamic leaders of the calibre of Muzadi and Ma'arif to overlook Ba'asyir's self-confessed militant radicalism so easily. While he was in jail in February 2003 Ba'asyir published *Dakwah & Jihad*, in which he reaffirmed his jihadi position and proudly proclaimed his hatred for the "United States and the Jews," writing: "One can expect being thwarted by the United

States, the world's terrorist nation, backed by the Jews, a race cursed by God." Using classic jihadi rhetoric, Ba'asyir urged Muslims to join in the holy struggle without fear of the consequences: "Even if one were to die as a result of this struggle, his death would not be in vain as he will be a martyr and be amply rewarded in heaven." Ba'asyir does not back away from his support of violence "when Islam is being attacked" and regularly articulates the militant Islamist jihadi interpretation of jihad, which justifies pre-emptive aggression, not simply self-defence. He openly and repeatedly urges young Muslim men to join in the violent struggle, as he has done for decades now, but is careful not to be seen directing them towards specific targets, making it difficult to attribute culpability to him for specific acts of violence. Ba'asyir walks a fine line, provoking his critics to accuse him but defying them to bring him down. In doing so he has succeeded, so far at least, in justifying the jihadi position and his "right" to incite violence in the name of Islam. He is reported to have said, "I make many knives, I sell many knives, but I am not responsible for how they are used."

It would be very wrong to interpret the scepticism of the moderate leaders of Nahdlatul Ulama and Muhammadiyah as evidence that they are condoning Ba'asyir's jihadi position. Nor are they like Vice-President Hamzah Haz, Ba'asyir's most senior friend and defender, who weeks before the cleric's arrest in October 2002 said, "if you want to arrest Abu Bakar Ba'asyir you will have to deal with me first." In 2002 Haz made a point of inviting Ba'asyir to dine in his vice-presidential office and of visiting him at his *pesantren* in Ngruki, on which occasion he observed: "there is no terrorist network in Indonesia, particularly in this school." Given this background it is not surprising that, although in recent months Hamzah Haz has wisely decided not to make any further public comments about Ba'asyir, he broke his silence after the verdict on Ba'asyir was announced by provocatively observing that "the US was the king of terrorism" and was maliciously trying to besmirch Indonesia's reputation by labelling it a "hotbed of terrorists."

There can be little doubt not only that Hamzah Haz, as leader of the conservative PPP (United Development Party), saw political gain in appealing to Ba'asyir's supporters ahead of the April 2004 general elections, but also that he is personally sympathetic to Ba'asyir's radical

Islamist ideological position. This is not in any way the case for either Hasyim Muzadi or Ahmad Syafi'i Ma'arif: their prevarication is indicative not so much of mainstream support for Ba'asyir and JI as of mainstream denial of the scale of the problem facing Indonesia. Ordinary Indonesians understandably feel that al-Qaeda-style jihadi Islamism is foreign to their society and their understanding of Islam. They also know that Indonesia has made excellent progress in pursuing those behind the Bali bombing, yet gets scant credit for this and continues to suffer criticism in the international media. After four decades of military-backed authoritarianism, replete with all manner of dirty-tricks operations and smear campaigns and one of the most corrupt and dysfunctional security and legal systems anywhere in the world, they are also understandably sceptical about the neat explanation being presented to them by the authorities for a string of mysterious bombings. Not surprisingly, ordinary Indonesians would rather not hear any more talk of terrorism and conspiratorial underground organisations, especially when the charges against Indonesia come from western governments, which they feel have been less than transparent about their dealings with the Muslim world and yet quick to shed blood in the name of "the war on terrorism." It is not surprising that a degree of denial has begun to take hold in Indonesia. None of this, however, will make Indonesia's problems go away. On the contrary, as long as the Indonesian government fails to deal systemically with the problem of terrorism, Indonesia continues to be vulnerable.

CHAPTER 4
The political struggle

Indonesia may be the world's largest Muslim nation but Islam in Indonesia has long been rather neglected by scholars of Islam and Indonesia alike. The view that Islam in Indonesia was somehow not authentic, and that its generally tolerant and relaxed character was a product of syncretism, became an established convention. Signs of liberality within Islam in Indonesia were seen as evidence that it was Indonesian society and culture, rather than Arab society and culture, that deviated from a true understanding of Islam. The religious character of Indonesian society, it was argued, should be understood as a work in progress. After all, Islam came relatively recently to the archipelago and fully penetrated the interior of Java only several centuries ago.

It is hard to argue with this perspective, especially as the social changes of the past three decades seem to bear it out. Nevertheless, it is too easy to overstate this and succumb to a reductionistic and essentialist teleology that simultaneously prejudices our understanding of progressive Islamic thought in Indonesia and, some would argue, blinds us to the dangers of creeping Islamist radicalism.

Is it time for us to reassess Indonesian Islam? To what extent does Indonesia face a threat from radical Islamists? Merely to articulate these questions is to raise the issue of normative judgement of differing interpretations of Islam – something about which many commentators, quite rightly, have grave concerns.

The tabloid press in the west does not, of course, display reservation in linking terms such as "fundamentalist," "terrorist" and "radical" to "Islam," nor do populist sections of the electronic media refrain from simplistic sensationalism. It is just as well, then, that more responsible agencies are now showing greater sensitivity in engaging with Muslim society. Nevertheless, this greater sensitivity is in itself no remedy if it is not accompanied by greater insight, and here the west is paying dearly for its previous lack of investment in understanding Islam and Muslim society.

As was discussed in chapter 2, at the core of the current problem is a historical failure to take Islamic thought seriously enough to study it deeply. Many western agencies now find themselves in a conceptual mire when it comes to understanding Islamic groups and movements, and they substitute simplistic prejudice for benign ignorance. Evidence for this can be found in reports of developments in Indonesia such as the remarkable electoral success of the Prosperous Justice Party (PKS) in the April 2004 parliamentary elections, the role of radical Islamist militias in communal violence in Maluku and Sulawesi, and the strong circumstantial evidence linking Abu Bakar Ba'asyir, Majelis Mujahidin Indonesia (MMI) and Jemaah Islamiyah (JI). The legitimate and reasonable fear of being seen to endorse the Islam-phobia of the tabloid press has sometimes resulted in a disinclination to critically examine the aspirations of radical Islamist groups.

Why this concern with political Islamism when this book is primarily concerned with the jihadi Islamism of Jemaah Islamiyah? Because the struggle to make Indonesia more Islamic needs to be understood in its totality. In one sense, all Muslims – Islamists and non-Islamists alike – agree that they have an obligation to conduct jihad to improve society and make the nation more truly Islamic. Where they differ from one another is in their understanding of what jihad means. Should their jihad, their struggle, be primarily in the realm of culture and society and philanthropy, or should it focus on the political sphere? And if it focuses on politics, then should the struggle be for the application of the Shariah or should it be for liberal democratic values (which can be understood as an embodiment of the principles of the Shariah)? If the struggle is for the literal application of the Shariah, then is it right to work with and through the existing nation state or should democracy and democratic means be totally rejected? And, finally, what means are permissible to achieve the ends that God intends?

The possibility of working together on a broad common front to Islamise Indonesian society might be rejected by moderates but is readily accepted by radicals. At the conclusion of their inaugural national congress on 7 August 2000, MMI delegates from across Indonesia signed their names to a declaration that they dubbed the Yogyakarta Charter (invoking remembrance of both the Medina Charter, described in the Qur'an, and the Jakarta Charter). After opening with a verse from the Qur'an the charter begins with:

> The Islamic community of Indonesia, representing an absolute majority of this nation, has both a right and a responsibility to establish and maintain Islamic law [the Sharia] as a consequence of the faith of which it is convinced. The Sharia is the one solution to all of the social, political and human crises that afflict the community of mankind. The protection of the faith of the religious community represents without exception the character of a government that is truly based on the Sharia. And so for that reason the preservation of the Sharia must become that which is above all else and preeminent and in all of the activities in the Muslim struggle. For surely the complete destruction of a people awaits them when they in ungodly ignorance turn away from following the Sharia.

The charter goes on to declare that the *mujahidin* agree together to: 1) apply the Shariah; 2) reject false ideology and the tyrannical abuse of human rights; 3) build up a strong local, regional and international *mujahidin* force; 4) work towards the realisation of a national and global caliphate; and 5) call on all Muslims to engage in jihad and *dakwah* (missionary activism).

The MMI congress was intended to unite all radical Islamists, whether in political parties or in social organisations, in a common struggle. The MMI as an organisation rejects the Indonesian government and all democratic institutions and processes as being contrary to the theocratic principles of Islam. Nevertheless, the MMI is clearly pleased to work with radical Islamist politicians and parties and even went as far as encouraging its members to vote in the 2004 elections and give their support to those parties most committed to the application of the Shariah. (This is interesting given the fact that the leaders of the Hizb ut-Tahrir community in Solo instructed their followers not to cast valid votes in the election.)

At one level, the various forms of radical Islamism need to be understood as existing on a broad continuum. And, to a significant extent, even where radical Islamists differ in their understanding of what means are permissible to achieve their ends, they interact with each other in a synergistic fashion. The MMI represents a point of contact between jihadi Islamism and radical political Islamism.

Were Indonesia in a situation of political stability and sustained economic growth, concerns about Islamist radicalism would be mitigated by the knowledge that radicalism would be kept in check by social and political forces. Unfortunately, Indonesia is still in the initial stages of regime change as the young nation attempts to break with four decades of military-backed authoritarianism and establish full democracy. Such transitions are not always successful, and even when they are, that success can remain very limited. It is, in large part, the fraught nature of the circumstances in which Indonesia finds itself today – midway on a journey to liberal democracy – that affords opportunities for Indonesia's small numbers of radical Islamists to influence society and politics to an extent out of all proportion to their true size.

Significant elements of the Soeharto regime – both institutions (few of which have changed significantly) and individuals – remain in power. Corruption ranks among the worst in the world (in a comprehensive report on 102 nations by Transparency International released in August 2002, Indonesia is perceived as being the seventh most corrupt nation in the world). Not only has little, if any, overall progress been made in fighting corruption since the fall of Soeharto more than five years ago, but there are also strong indications that, in certain areas, corruption has become even worse. Moves to decentralise government, although begun with good intentions under B. J. Habibie's interim presidency, were ill-conceived and the transition poorly managed, further exacerbating rentier capitalism and endemic corruption in the regions, with the orderly and centralised corruption of the Soeharto era replaced by a chaotic free-for-all. At the same time, members of parliament, who now wield real power, and senior bureaucrats have become increasingly rapacious and accustomed to a dramatic inflation in the payments required to lubricate the wheels of progress.

This corruption is both a product of a weak legal system and an obstacle to serious judicial reform. Consequently, rule of law is incomplete at best, and non-existent at worst. International observers watching the trials of the Bali bombers in Denpasar, Bali, witnessed a display of rare professionalism and transparency. But what many did not realise was just how untypical these trials were. As Indonesia's struggle with terrorism moves beyond the initial phase of post-Bali arrests, there is a real danger that subsequent trials will not prove so satisfactory. One factor that could influence future trials is the possibility that investigations into JI and other militant Islamist groups could uncover matters that elements of the military would rather not have brought into the open. At this point there is no evidence that the Indonesian military is involved with JI; nor is there any reason to imagine that direct links exist. Unlike Laskar Jihad, JI is opposed to all forms of secular government and its institutions, and is therefore ideologically opposed to working with the Indonesian military. This is not to say that some groups and individuals currently associated with JI do not have past dealings with individuals within TNI (the Indonesian armed forces). Indeed, it would be very unlikely that no such secondary links exist. Given the way in which elements of the military are able to distort and direct legal proceedings when their interests are at stake – as the disappointing lack of prosecutions relating to military-related violence in East Timor in 1999 makes abundantly clear – there are strong grounds for being concerned about future proceedings that deal with terrorists.

Despite its commitment to withdraw from the parliament in 2004, the military remains outside civil control. Elements of the military continue to abuse human rights, and the institution as a whole, for reasons over which it does not have full control, remains deeply enmeshed in organised criminality on multiple fronts. This means that many of the basic incentives and pressures that drove the military to exploit radical Islamist militias in recent years continue.

Leaving aside for the moment the political machinations of the Indonesian elite, what can we say about the attitudes and convictions of ordinary Indonesians? The only reliable, and indeed the only consequential, polling of the opinions of ordinary Indonesians across the archipelago is that which has taken place in Indonesia's three free and fair national elections over the past five decades.

In March 1945 the Japanese allowed the nationalists to begin formulating the political structure for an independent Indonesia. Sharp disagreements about the role of Islam saw the discussions bog down, and in June Sukarno proposed a compromise that would recognise the role of religion without threatening non-*santri* (non-practising) Muslims and religious minorities. The result was the *panca sila* (usually referred to as Pancasila), the "five principles" (Sukarno used the Sanskrit terminology to impose a bit of gravitas and imply deep historical roots), the first *sila* of which spoke vaguely of "belief in God." This provoked consternation among Islamic leaders and they countered with the addition of seven words so that the first *sila* became: "belief in God with the obligation for adherents of Islam to carry out the Sharia." This formulation became known as the Jakarta Charter and from the very beginning met with fierce resistance from many within the nationalist movement. In the wake of the Japanese surrender, independence was formally declared on 17 August 1945. The next day Sukarno and Mohammad Hatta relented in the face of robust protests and dropped the Jakarta Charter. By way of a compromise brokered by Wahid Hasyim and other Nahdlatul Ulama (NU) leaders, the first *sila* was changed to read: "belief in God Who is one," in accordance with the Islamic (and Christian) doctrine of *tauhid*, or the one-ness of God.

Initially, modernist Muslims from Muhammadiyah and Persis and traditionalist Muslims from NU had worked together within Masyumi. But in 1952 the rusticated traditionalists, fed up with being considered inferior to their urban modernist coreligionists, split from Masyumi and NU formed their own political party. Throughout the Japanese occupation and the post-war revolutionary struggle, the modernists and traditionalists had worked side by side with a reasonable degree of success. The issue that had proven most divisive among the Muslim political elite during these formative years was not the decades-old modernist–traditionalist divide but the question of what role Islam should play in the new nation. Like Sukarno, NU leader Wahid Hasyim favoured a "secular," or at least non-sectarian, state philosophy. Many of his peers within NU, however, were social conservatives and argued that Islam should be recognised as the basis of the Indonesian state. Masyumi leader Mohammad Natsir, who, significantly, came from the small, conservative, modernist organisation Persis, and was strongly

Table 1: Performance of major parties in the 1955 election

Party	Orientation	Notes	% valid votes	% seats
Masyumi	modernist *santri*	mix of radical & moderate Islamists, & pluralists	20.9	22.2
NU	traditionalist *santri*	mix of radical & moderate Islamists, & pluralists	18.4	17.5
PNI	secular nationalist	initially close to Sukarno	22.3	22.2
PKI	Communist	opposed by *santri* Muslims and ABRI	16.4	15.2
Total of 4 major parties			78.0	77.1

influenced by the writing of Maududi, argued that the new nation should be formally based on Islam. Nevertheless, many of his colleagues in Masyumi were prepared to accept the compromise theistic nonsectarian-secularism of Pancasila.

The controversy surrounding the dropping of the Jakarta Charter refused to dissipate. When an election was finally held in 1955, the reintroduction of the Jakarta Charter, and its attendant implication of applying the Shariah, became a major issue in the campaign. Four parties polled strongly and garnered almost 80 per cent of the vote. But Islamic leaders were disappointed because Masyumi (with 20.9 per cent) and NU (with 18.4 per cent) collected just under 40 per cent of the vote, meaning that support for political Islam fell well short of a majority (see table 1, above). The issue of the Jakarta Charter dominated the deliberations of the post-election Constituent Assembly that was to draft a complete new constitution, and ultimately contributed to the demise of both the assembly and parliamentary democracy at the hands of Sukarno. During the following decades, the struggle to make the nation Islamic became an obsession for the modernists and came to dominate modernist thought.

In 1958 Natsir and other Masyumi leaders participated in regional rebellions in the Darul Islam stronghold of South Sulawesi and in the religious conservative province of West Sumatra (Natsir's home province). For their efforts they were rewarded with the formal banning of Masyumi in January 1960, an experience that drove Islamist modernists such as Natsir closer to the position of the Darul Islam activists. In response to further frustration under the military-backed Soeharto regime, which was strongly disinclined to permit an Islamist party as strong as Masyumi ever to form again, and inspired by Maududi's vision of *dakwah* as jihad, Natsir set up Dewan Dakwah Islamiyah Indonesia (DDII). In time DDII was to give rise to the even more radically Islamist Indonesia Committee for Solidarity with the Muslim World (KISDI).

After a rather messy election in 1971, the first national poll since 1955, Soeharto decided that it was time to simplify the political system. In 1973 he declared that, henceforth, there would be only two opposition parties: one Islamic party, the United Development Party (PPP), and one secular-nationalist party, the Indonesian Democratic Party (PDI). No one imagined for a minute that any party but Soeharto's Golkar would form government.

When Indonesia's first free and fair election since 1955 was finally held in June 1999, a year after Soeharto's departure, it was surprising how little things had changed in 44 years. In 1999 the proportion of the combined national vote achieved by the Islamic parties was 38 per cent (see table 2, overleaf), virtually the same result as was achieved by Masyumi and NU in 1955. But one thing that had changed was that the parties which depended on support from *santri* Muslims fell into two clear camps. The NU-backed National Awakening Party (PKB) of Abdurrahman Wahid (with 12.6 per cent) and the Muhammadiyah-backed National Mandate Party (PAN) of Amien Rais (with 7.1 per cent), which together garnered almost 20 per cent of the vote, were self-consciously non-Islamist, pluralist parties. Hamzah Haz's PPP (with 10.7 per cent), the Crescent Moon and Star Party (PBB) of Yusril Izha Mahendra (with 1.9 per cent), and the Justice Party (PK) of Hidayat Nur Wahid (with 1.4 per cent), on the other hand, identified as Islamist parties, the former being more moderate and the latter two more radical. Although only PPP, drawing on its Soeharto-era legacy of habitual voters, managed to obtain a sizeable share of the vote by itself, these three Islamist parties, joined by several smaller Islamist parties, together achieved 18 per cent of the national vote.

Some commentators speak about a decline in the Islamist vote from 1955 to 1999 but that interpretation makes the mistake of assuming that Masyumi and NU supporters were all voting for Islamist parties. In fact both parties had radical Islamist and moderate Islamist, as well as non-Islamist, politicians (with Masyumi having rather more of the former), making direct comparisons between 1955 and 1999 difficult.

Not surprisingly, it is much easier to compare results between the 1999 and 2004 elections. Most commentators were not surprised to see a significant decline in support for Megawati's PDIP in 2004, although few predicted that the decline would be quite so dramatic. Even more surprising is where the disgruntled former PDIP supporters took their votes. It had been expected that Golkar would be the primary beneficiary of PDIP's fall to earth. Instead two small parties, the Prosperous Justice Party (PKS, effectively a reformulation of PK) of Hidayat Nur Wahid (with 7.2 per cent) and the Democratic Party (Partai Demokrat) of Susilo Bambang Yudhoyono (with 7.5 per cent) appeared to have received a windfall from voters fleeing PDIP.

The amazing success of the Democratic Party, which did not even exist in 1999, can largely be explained by the popularity of Yudhoyono and the fact that many Indonesians wished to see this reform-minded former four-star general, whom they see to be clean, capable and strong, become their next president. While Yudhoyono's 34 per cent of the vote in the first round of the presidential elections on 5 July was well below what polling had predicted, it was still well ahead of Megawati's 26 per cent and built impressively on his own party's vote in the parliamentary election.

The appeal of the hard-working, highly professional PKS is more difficult to explain. Voter support for the party, which had hoped to achieve as much as 4 per cent of the vote, exceeded even its own expectations. In the national capital PKS polled more than any other party, with 22 per cent of the vote, just ahead of the Democratic Party with 20 per cent. For many urban voters it seems likely that both parties enjoyed a similar appeal, regarded as free of corruption and genuinely commit-

Table 2: Performance of the major parties in the 1999 and 2004

Party	Leader/ key figure	Orientation	Notes	1999 % votes
Golkar	Wiranto/Tandjung	secular nationalist	Indonesia wide	22.4
PDIP	Megawati	secular nationalist	Java/Bali strength	33.7
Partai Demokrat	Susilo B. Yudhoyono	secular nationalist	Indonesia wide	–
PDS		secular nationalist	Christian party	–
Sub-total of secular nationalist parties				56.1
PKB	A. Wahid	pluralist Islam NU masses	dependent on Wahid (Gus Dur)	12.6
PAN	Amien Rais	pluralist Islam Muhammadiyah	now arguably less liberal	7.1
Sub-total of secular Muslim parties				19.7
PPP	Hamzah Haz	moderate Islamist	radical Islamist element	10.7
PBR	Zainuddin MZ	moderate Islamist	breakaway from PPP	–
PBB	Yusril Mahendra	radical Islamist	Yusril influential in cabinet 1999–2005	1.9
PKS	Hidayat Nur Wahid	radical Islamist	renamed in 2003: previously PK	1.4
Sub-total of Islamist parties				14/ 18**
Total of all Islamic parties				37.7**
Grand total of all major parties				89.8

Notes: * 462 elected representatives and 38 TNI appointees

elections

1999 seats* (462+38)	2004 % votes	2004 seats (550)
118 23.6%	21.6	128 23.3%
151 30.2%	18.5	109 19.8%
–	7.5	57 10.4%
–	2.1	12 2.2%
269 53.8%	49.7	306 55.6%
51 10.2%	10.6	52 9.5%
34 6.8%	6.4	52 9.5%
85 17.0%	17.0	104 18.9%
58 11.6%	8.2	58 10.5%
–	2.8	13 2.4%
13 2.6%	2.6	11 2.0%
7 1.4%	7.2	45 8.2%
78 15.6%	20.8	127 23.1%
163 32.6%	37.8	231 42.0%
432 86.4%	87.5	537 97.6%

** totals including minor parties

ted to reform. PKS was also widely seen to be very professional in the way it managed its cadre system and to be fostering a culture of meritocracy in which younger activists were given real opportunities to prove themselves – something that was not to be found in any of the other parties.

It is these appealing characteristics that commentators have pointed to in attempting to explain how the total percentage of the Islamist party vote went from 14 per cent (for PPP, PBB and PK) in 1999 to 21 per cent in 2004. But this line of analysis overlooks the fact that in 1999, when 48 parties contested the election – twice as many as in 2004 – a significant scatter of votes went to very small Islamist parties. At 18 per cent, the total vote of all Islamist parties combined in 1999 is still 3 per cent less than the vote achieved by Islamist parties in 2004, but not so very different. Considering the breakdown of votes in Jakarta, it seems reasonable to draw the conclusion that the 3 per cent gain can be credited to former PDIP voters being attracted to PKS's clean, professional image. Nevertheless, the rest of PKS's gain should probably be understood as representing a consolidation of the radical Islamist vote into one party.

This last point is very significant because, if correct, it would mean that despite the fact that PKS tried to deflect attention from its radical-Islamist agenda it was still able to draw a strong core of voters sympathetic to those aims. This knowledge is likely to influence the parliamentary behaviour of the PKS and PBB, which hold 10 per cent of the seats, and to some extent PPP and PBR, which hold a further 13 per cent.

•

The debate about the role religion should play in Indonesia has been fiercely contested from the time it became a nation. Despite what the bare demographic figures might suggest, that contest is far from over. In the freedom of the post-Soeharto era, the contest is once again out in the open. Even with modest support in the 1999 election, the radical Islamists have proven themselves remarkably successful in building their influence in the government and legislature. Led by the PBB chairman and justice minister, Yusril Izha Mahendra, they succeeded in introducing two new bills to the legislature that, if passed, would dramatically curtail individual freedoms. The first of these is the revised Criminal Code, which contains controversial new laws criminalising adultery, oral sex, cohabitation and homosexuality. When questioned about the bill in October 2003, Yusril, who makes no secret of his long-standing intention to use the legislature to introduce the Shariah one piece at a time, acknowledged that the new Criminal Code would help bring Indonesian law more into line with the Shariah on sexual matters. Indeed, he urged a gathering of MMI leaders in West Java in 2003 to support his efforts in the political arena, promising them that he was working towards the very same ends as they were.

The second piece of proposed legislation, the bill on religious tolerance, which has been criticised by both Muhammadiyah and NU but welcomed by the Islamist and non-representative Council of Indonesian Ulama (MUI), is even more alarming in its scope. (The MUI encourages the press to describe it as being "Indonesia's peak body of *ulama*" but in reality the MUI is but a cynical creation of the Soeharto regime that has little contact with the vast majority of *ulama*, who are affiliated with NU.) This bill would make proselytising and conversion illegal, would prohibit inter-religious marriage, would place a legal obligation on Muslims to "commemorate religious holidays" (requiring the state to police fasting during Ramadan) and would outlaw deviant religious teaching. In other words, if passed, it would effectively represent an introduction of the Jakarta Charter by the back door. The insidious consequences of this sort of legislation can be readily seen in Pakistan, where successive military governments have pandered to Pakistan's radical Islamist minority in an attempt to buy its support.

Drawing attention to the Pakistan experience sometimes provokes a sharp reaction from observers of Indonesia, who argue that radical Islamism has very little support in Indonesian society and will clearly never achieve a political majority. The suggestion that the situation in Pakistan is markedly different from that in Indonesia is curious. In fact, radical Islamist parties have historically had less popular support in Pakistan than they have in Indonesia. It is interesting to note that in the 2002 elections in Pakistan, in which the MMA, a coalition of six radical Islamist parties, was seen to have achieved unprecedented electoral support, its share of votes was still only 11 per cent, or just over half the level of support achieved by all Islamist parties in Indonesia in 2004, and barely higher than the 10 per cent achieved by Indonesia's radical Islamist parties PKS and PBB.

Until very recently the proposition that Indonesia might go the way of Pakistan would have been readily rejected by most observers. But if these two new bills are passed in anything like their current form, Indonesia would already be starting to resemble Pakistan in the tyranny of an extremist minority over a moderate majority in relation to religious freedoms. This realisation should have us questioning the nature of the relationship between political Islamism and jihadi Islamism in Indonesia. For while there is no simple, direct relationship between the two, the experience of Pakistan suggests that they interact synergistically. In other words, what benefits one tends to benefit the other.

To some extent this dynamic has already been seen in Indonesia, too, where the fear of a backlash from political Islamists has greatly impeded official efforts to tackle JI and jihadi Islamism. If the parallel with Pakistan holds, even in part, it would mean that Indonesia's problems with jihadi extremism are only just beginning.

CHAPTER 5
Responding to radical Islamism

Some important questions, unpalatable though they may be, now need to be asked. Is Jemaah Islamiyah a stand-alone phenomenon or are the socio-economic conditions and the political environment in post-Soeharto Indonesia such that radical Islamism is able to steadily ratchet up its influence? If the latter is the case, are elements within the military opportunistically supporting radical Islamist militias? Are elements of the political elite showing signs of exploiting the appeal of radical Islamist ideas as a way of leveraging their political power without regard for social consequences?

It might be argued that such a speculative approach is unjustified and that discussion should be limited to matters clearly and unambiguously supported by hard evidence. Unquestionably, the Polri–AFP investigation into the Bali bombing proved the worth of such an evidentiary approach when it led to the eventual arrest of hundreds of suspects and the successful prosecution of the bombers. There are clear limits, however, to the issues that a police-style investigation can deal with. The sort of analysis that is required to anticipate the further development of jihadi terrorism in Southeast Asia is necessarily much more speculative. It certainly needs to be happening in the intelligence community, but it should also be taking place more broadly among academics and other observers.

If militant religious extremism in Indonesia were being expressed only through JI, at least the parameters of the problem could be understood and the issue addressed. Moreover, if JI were solely a product of a foreign Islamic militancy that had found limited acceptance in Indonesia through the unique circumstances of Indonesian *mujahidin* returning home from radicalising experiences in Afghanistan and Pakistan, we could find comfort in the hope that Jemaah Islamiyah and jihadi Islamism were but a temporary aberration that has already begun to wane. There is certainly much truth in such analysis but the reality is, nevertheless, rather more complex.

The threat posed by jihadi Islamism in Indonesia is both more insidious and more far-reaching than JI's involvement in the Bali bombing suggests. The death toll of 202 in Bali may have been significantly smaller than the September 11 attack in the United States, but by any other measure the 12 October 2002 Bali bombing, like the 11 March 2004 bomb attacks in Madrid, was a major terrorist event. If we add to this the dozens killed in the many earlier bombings now known to have been the work of JI, including the Christmas Eve bombings of 2000 and the Marriott bombing ten months after Bali, the death toll swells still further. Even so, if this were the full extent of the problem, it could be argued that the western media is exaggerating the threat beyond its true proportions and that in any case, with over 200 JI operatives across Southeast Asia now in detention, including most of JI's senior leadership, the threat posed by JI is now receding. By that argument, it could be said that after JI has done its worst in terms of loss of life, the outcome is no graver than that of the sinking of a passenger ferry, and we have, after all, become accustomed to hundreds of lives being lost in Indonesia every year through such accidents. From a somewhat different point of view, it could be argued that even if JI does regenerate and rebuild, the threat it poses to Indonesia is similar in nature to that posed to Spanish society in recent decades by the Basque separatist group, ETA. In other words, it could be argued that JI is a discrete threat involving a tiny proportion of citizens and is without broad appeal, or indeed relevance. But the reality is not so palatable and not nearly so simple.

We now know that JI is not simply an imported problem; rather it is, in part, a continuation of the Darul Islam struggle of the 1950s. Moreover, JI is involved in many more deaths than those caused by bombings; and it is not the only militant radical Islamist organisation committed to carrying out jihad in Indonesia. Since 2000, at least 5000, and some would say as many as 10,000, people have been killed in Maluku (including the South Maluku capital of Ambon). Another

2000 or more lives have been lost in recent years in the city of Poso and surrounding areas in Central Sulawesi. These communal conflicts have organic origins in socioeconomic cleavages and related tensions and are not quintessentially religious conflicts. Nevertheless, the JI militias Laskar Mujahidin and Laskar Jundullah, and affiliates such as Mujahidin KOMPAK, together with competing radical Islamist militias such as Laskar Jihad, have greatly exacerbated the conflicts, and have been directly involved in the deaths of thousands of people.

If this were all the work of underground terrorist groups rejected by mainstream society it would be bad enough. But Abu Bakar Ba'asyir's Majelis Mujahidin Indonesia (MMI) openly campaigns to send *mujahidin* to Maluku and Central Sulawesi. Moreover, it has sought and received the support of mainstream Islamist parties and Islamist leaders. At the same time, political leaders as senior as justice and human rights minister Yusril Izha Mahendra and vice-president Hamzah Haz have openly and vigorously campaigned for Ba'asyir.

Sadly, we now do need to raise the question of whether there is a real danger, however remote, that Indonesia will follow the path of Pakistan. In other words, will a small radical Islamist minority, aided and abetted by opportunistic elements within the civil and military elite, and by deteriorating economic and social conditions, come to disturb the religious and political freedoms of a moderate majority, particularly in outlying provinces? As we saw in chapter 1, the Bali bombing investigation led to a series of arrests and discoveries that greatly extended our knowledge of Jemaah Islamiyah. Most of what was discussed in chapter 3 was learnt in the wake of the Bali bombing investigation. If that Bali transport authority registration number had not been discovered by General Pastika's colleague and the link to Amrozi not established, then it is likely that further atrocities would have occurred, perhaps in the weeks after the Bali bombing and almost certainly in the year that followed; and not just in Indonesia but elsewhere in Southeast Asia as well. Without that initial breakthrough, dangerous JI leaders such as Imam Samudra and Hambali would probably not have been arrested, and weapons and explosives such as those in the large cache found in Semarang in July 2003 (160 kg of TNT, 900 kg of potassium chlorate, 1000 detonators, 65 PETN high-explosive detonators, timers and batteries, maps and planning documents, eleven shoulder-launched rockets and several M16s together with 22,000 rounds of ammunition) would have probably been used to take many lives, possibly repeating the tragedy in Bali several times over. Instead it appears that good work by Indonesian authorities and their partners in the region has greatly diminished the immediate threat posed by JI. At the very least, it appears that both JI's capacity and its political will to carry out further bombing "spectaculars" aimed at large-scale indiscriminate killing and maiming have, for the immediate future at least, been significantly reduced.

Unfortunately, this good news also contains the seeds of bad news. JI's scope to act has been greatly curtailed but the organisation is by no means finished. It is disturbing that the Indonesian government has still not moved to ban JI and that leading politicians, including even stalwart opponents of JI such as Susilo Bambang Yudhoyono, continue to deny that banning JI is possible or even desirable.

Even during these most difficult of times for JI, when the network has been critically weakened and is under close surveillance, there is evidence that it continues to play a role in exacerbating communal violence in Central Sulawesi, and possibly in Maluku. As the International Crisis Group's Sidney Jones has observed, a weakened JI no longer under strong central control may transmute into an even more dangerous presence on the ground in regions such as Sulawesi, as less well-trained and disciplined operatives create mayhem in remote communities. Given the scale of suffering, it may be that this contribution to promoting communal violence actually represents a more serious threat than the sort of attacks that preoccupy the international media. If the next five years see thousands more lives lost in such violence in eastern Indonesia, few outside Indonesia may notice but the scale of human suffering would be far worse than that caused by several more bombing spectaculars like the one of 12 October 2002.

It would also be a serious error to discount the possibility of JI's mounting further large-scale attacks. Indeed, there now appears reason to believe that JI has already been indirectly involved in another bombing that has killed hundreds of people. Moments before they died, the seven al-Qaeda operatives who blew themselves up in their flat in Leganes, South Madrid, on 3 April 2004, tried three times to telephone jailed al-Qaeda leader Abu Qatada. They were apparently seeking the permission of the alleged leader of al-Qaeda in Britain, who was being detained in London's Belmarsh prison, to commit suicide rather than allow themselves to be captured. Several of the men were wanted by the police in connection with the 11 March train bombings in Madrid in which 191 people were killed. Telephone records reveal that they also tried to call a JI leader close to Abu Bakar Ba'asyir. According to Sidney Jones, a number of the al-Qaeda members in Spain had been trained at a JI camp near Poso, and links between the al-Qaeda cell in Spain and JI in Indonesia went back at least as far as 2000. Abu Dahdah himself, the alleged leader of al-Qaeda's Spanish operation, visited Poso in May 2001. And in the critical Semarang raid in July 2003, Indonesian police found, together with the explosives and numerous weapons, two copies of the Qur'an in Spanish, another Spanish book and 26 Spanish business cards.

For some time Singaporean authorities have been openly expressing their fears that terrorists might seize control of an oil or gas supertanker in the Strait of Malacca, or in other waterways near Singapore, the world's busiest port, with the intent of turning it into a floating bomb. Thirty per cent of the world's traded goods and 80 per cent of Japan's crude oil pass through the Strait of Malacca, and the poorly policed narrow waterway is the world's number one location for pirate attacks. One hundred and twenty-one pirate attacks were recorded in Indonesian waters in 2003, along with a further 35 in Malaysian and Singaporean waters. In recent years a number of tug boats have been hijacked and stolen and on several occasions "pirates" have seized control of vessels for several hours, apparently purely with the intent of learning how to steer the ships. There is good reason to believe that even a severely weakened JI might still be capable of exploding a supertanker in the vicinity of Singapore.

In the longer term, the capacity of JI to regenerate with new recruits should not be underestimated. Enough of JI's senior leaders and operatives remain at large to oversee the rebuilding of the organisation. As well, the current high levels of anger against the west among radical Islamist communities in Indonesia, exacerbated by the protracted conflict in Iraq and bad news from the Middle East, mean that JI will find it relatively easy to attract new *mujahidin* to join in its struggle. Training new members does not present JI with any great problems either. Even though only a trickle of trainees appears to have passed through the Moro Islamic Liberation Front's training camps in Mindanao since the Bali bombing, limited training has been occurring in Sulawesi. It is still relatively easy for JI recruits to blend in with the tens of thousands of Southeast Asians travelling to Pakistan and the Middle East every year, so there is no reason why new JI operatives could not be trained in Pakistan or Afghanistan.

In short, JI may have been critically weakened but it continues to represent a significant threat, not least in areas prone to communal violence in eastern Indonesia, and it should be expected that it will steadily rebuild its strength. The jihadi Islamist vision of JI and its affiliates is a long-term one, and one that inspires deep commitment; consequently there is every reason to regard JI, or future mutations of it, as a significant threat for the foreseeable future.

•

Given that Indonesia's tiny minority of jihadi Islamists remain a substantial threat, and that radical Islamists in general are determined to continue their struggle to make Indonesian society more Islamic, what sort of response is required? In trying to determine the issues that need to be focused on and the parameters of the challenge facing us, we need to start with the seminal ideas. But before we reflect on the specifics of jihadi Islamism we need to back up a little and reassess our understanding of Islam in general.

In this post–September 11 age of "war on terrorism," the widespread ignorance of Islam in the west can no longer be regarded as inconsequential. Now more than ever we need to understand the variegated complexity of a religion that shapes the lives of 1.3 billion people living in a band of contiguous nation states stretching halfway around the globe. It is no longer acceptable for us to talk of Islam in monolithic terms. Finding the right language with which to begin to understand the rich diversity of Muslim practices and attitudes is crucial if we are not to fall into habitual errors of reductionism and essentialism when talking about Islam and Muslim society.

One of the most clear-cut and influential examples of essentialist thinking about Islam is found in Samuel Huntington's clash-of-civilisations thesis. Huntington does not mince words:

Some Westerners, including President Bill Clinton, have argued that the West does not have problems with Islam but only with violent Islamist extremists. Fourteen hundred years of history demonstrate otherwise. The relations between Islam and Christianity, both Orthodox and Western, have often been stormy. Each has been the other's Other. The twentieth-century conflict between liberal democracy and Marxist-Leninism is only a fleeting and superficial historical phenomenon compared to the continuing and deeply conflictual relation between Islam and Christianity. At times, peaceful coexistence has prevailed; more often the relation has been one of intense rivalry and of varying degrees of hot war...

The underlying problem for the West is not Islamic fundamentalism. It is Islam, a different civilization whose people are convinced of the superiority of their culture and are obsessed with the inferiority of their power. The problem for Islam is not the CIA or the U.S. Department of Defense. It is the West, a different civilization whose people are convinced of the universality of their culture and believe that their superior, if declining power imposes on them the obligation to extend that culture throughout the world. These are the basic ingredients that fuel conflict between Islam and the West.

Huntington paints with confidence on a broad canvas and the image he creates is seductively attractive in its simplicity. He is by no means alone.

There is much of value in Huntington's book, not least its challenge to take culture and civilisation seriously. Central to what I argue in this book, however, is that indeed "the West does not have problems with Islam but only with violent Islamist extremists." It pains me to write at length about Islamist extremism precisely because I do not see Islam as being a problem in itself. There is no doubt that Islam in principle supports tolerance and mutual respect in the face of social pluralism, and the actual experience of Islam in Indonesia regularly proves this in practice. The sort of militant radicalism expressed by jihadi groups like Jemaah Islamiyah, Laskar Jundullah, Laskar Jihad and so forth is at odds with the general mood of Muslim society in Indonesia and these groups are but a tiny minority among Indonesia's 200 million Muslims. Nevertheless, Indonesia does have a serious problem. Indonesia is in the midst of a struggle to determine who speaks for the soul of Islam.

Ironically, while most Muslim scholars argue that Samuel Huntington is basically wrong about Islam, radical Islamists agree completely with his proposition. Huntington's mistake is to describe the entire Muslim world in terms that really only apply to its radical Islamist minority. Sadly, so strident is the voice of this minority and so quick are they to claim to speak in the name of Islam (MUI is a classic example of this) that western observers such as Huntington can easily mistake them to be representing the "silent majority."

When the seminal ideas of jihadi Islamism are considered it is clear that Indonesian Islam has been globalised to an extent and in a manner not previously recognised. Jihadi Islamism, born of the union of the totalism of twentieth-century thinkers such as Sayyid Qutb and the proselytising exclusivism of Wahhabism, has clearly now joined the ideas of Muhammad Abduh, Rashid Rida and Maududi in shaping Islamic thought and conviction in Indonesia for a significant section of the *umat* (Muslim community). The essentialist argument that "Indonesian Islam is different" is no longer a tenable response to concerns about the reach of Islamist extremism into the Malay world. Moreover, the hopeful refrain that political Islamism is unrelated to jihadi Islamism must give way to an acknowledgement that, whatever their differences, the fact that they share some ideas must necessarily produce some common sympathies. This is not to say that the radical political Islamists are not being sincere when they speak of rejecting the methods of terrorism, but rather that for all their differences, radical political and jihadi Islamism relate to each other synergistically. This has clearly been the case in Pakistan and there is mounting evidence that it is also so in Indonesia.

If we are to understand the powerful appeal of Qutb's revolutionary ideas we need to try to read them from the inside looking out. To do this is to begin to see the beauty of Qutb's thought to those who have fallen under its spell. As Paul Berman astutely observes:

> Qutb's analysis was rich, nuance deep, soulful, and heartfelt. The analysis did not rest on two or three simple factors, the way that nineteenth-century analyses sometimes did. It was a theological analysis, but, in its

cultural emphases, it had twentieth-century style. The analysis asked some authentically perplexing questions – about the division between mind and body in Western thought; about the difficulties in striking a practical balance between sensual experience and spiritual elevation; about the soullessness of modern power; about technological innovation; about social justice.

American hypocrisy exercised him; but only slightly. His deepest quarrel was not with America's failure to uphold its principles. His quarrel was with the principles. He opposed the United States because it was a liberal society, and not because it failed to be a liberal society.

The truly dangerous element in American life was not capitalism or foreign policy, or racism, or the exploitation of women. The truly dangerous part lay in the separation of Church and State.

His fear was, instead, that liberal doctrines about religion would spread from the Western societies into the Muslim world, and take root there, and crowd out Islam. He worried that liberal ideas would penetrate the Muslim mind.

Berman's observations go to the heart of radical Islamism. The central passion driving radical Islamism, both political Islamism and jihadi Islamism, is the need for God to be over all. Ironically it is all about religion and yet, take away the religious language and it is clearly recognisable as another manifestation of that great twentieth-century creation: utopian totalitarianism. Although jihadi Islamism sees itself as struggling against godless materialism and returning society to true religion, it represents, in fact, a profoundly materialistic, anti-spiritual understanding of religion.

The struggle against radical Islamism needs to be fought on a number of levels but the first of these is the level of ideas. It is only by progressive Islamic writers making clear, with the same passion and eloquence demonstrated by the radical Islamists, the profound ways in which the underlying message of Islam is congruent with liberal, democratic values, that the powerful attraction of radical Islamist thought can be countered in the marketplace of ideas.

Because radical Islamism, in its roots, is a religious movement even more than it is a political movement, one of the effective ways to counter the threats posed by both political Islamism and jihadi

Islamism is to win the support and confidence of the moderate Muslim mainstream and strengthen the hand of Islamic liberals. As was noted at the beginning of this book, there are worrying signs that the tide of public opinion in Indonesia may once again be turning. The moderate majority in Indonesia, who only began to be persuaded in 2003 that jihadi Islamism in the form of Jemaah Islamiyah represented a genuine, home-grown threat, are now beginning to have second thoughts.

Indonesia's Islamic liberals, like the radical Islamists who oppose them, represent a small but critically important minority of Indonesian Muslims and, also like the radical Islamists, their influence on broader Muslim society can be catalytic. Each group feels locked in battle to shift the centre of gravity within Muslim society. All things being equal, the liberals would probably continue to make steady gains, as they did in the 1970s and 1980s when Soeharto stayed the hand of the Islamists and thus allowed the nascent Islamic liberalism movement to develop and strike roots in Indonesian society. Today, however, all things are not equal. The current global environment is one factor that might well work to the advantage of the radical Islamists, especially if the "war on terrorism" produces a significant "blow back" effect.

The liberals face four other factors that serve to constrain them and limit their effectiveness. First, the radical Islamists make effective use of intimidation to stop the liberals getting their message out through the media. There have been many incidents where militant Islamists have enjoyed great success by using mob violence to intimidate media companies into changing course. The Chinese Catholic publishing consortium Gramedia, whose publications include the national dailies *Kompas* and the *Jakarta Post*, has suffered from highly effective campaigns of intimidation. More recently, prominent young liberal Islamic intellectual Ulil Abshar Abdalla and his Liberal Islamic Network group have seen their public-service television advertisement proclaiming "Islam is multi-coloured" (*Islam warna-warni*) pulled from broadcast in the face of pressure from the Indonesian Mujahidin Council (MMI) of Abu Bakar Ba'asyir.

More dramatically, and far more significantly, in December 2002 Ulil received the unfortunate distinction of becoming the first Indonesian Islamic intellectual in the modern period to be the subject of a fatwa, albeit one from a little-known group, authorising his death on the grounds of apostasy because of an article that he wrote in *Kompas*.

Secondly, liberal Muslim groups require extensive capacity-building, as they tend to be less well organised, resourced and managed compared to the radical Islamists. In particular, where radical Islamists have long realised the benefit of networking, both locally and globally, liberal Islamic activists are comparatively poorly networked.

Thirdly, certain radical Islamists enjoy strong party-political and military connections and support. In part this has to do with their utility to elite power-brokers during this period of regime change and transition. This affords them a considerable degree of freedom to act and consequently amplifies their capacity to intimidate their opponents.

Fourthly, while both the radical Islamists and Islamic liberals have a catalytic influence over Muslim society, the related "ratchet effect" of such influence tends to work much more strongly in favour of the radicals. In other words, gains made by radical Islamists are very difficult to reverse and over time the cumulative effect of a series of small gains can be considerable, whereas gains made by liberals are much more easily lost. The critical thing to watch now is the manner and extent to which jihadi Islamism and political Islamism influence each other. The critical challenge is to disengage these two very different Islamisms from each other and limit their ability to persuade moderate Muslims who are feeling confused, anxious and fatigued to the point of depression about Indonesia's crisis-ridden state, the failure of reform and the criticism from the international community.

The pattern of history points to the fact that, even if it only directly affects a minute fraction of Indonesian society, the advent of Jemaah Islamiyah–al-Qaeda–style jihadi Islamism in the Indonesian archipelago marks a sea change in Indonesian Islam. The Padri movement in nineteenth-century West Sumatra and the Darul Islam rebellion in 1950s West Java both contained significant elements of antecedent forms of jihadi Islamism, but they were nevertheless very local in their concerns. The jihadi Islamism that Indonesia is experiencing today is global in orientation; it very much subscribes to the injunction to "think globally, act locally."

This modern form of globalised and globalising jihadi Islamism had its genesis in the *mujahidin* struggle in Afghanistan and in the related training camps and *madrasah* of Pakistan. So the key to understanding Indonesia's jihadi Islamist networks is first to understand the networks formed by the "Afghanistan alumni," and the ways in which these networks have been reinforced through marriage and through the associated network of jihadi *madrasah* and *pesantren*.

Of no less importance is the need to learn the lesson of the Afghanistan experience and be alert and responsive to the possibility that the radicalising experience of the *mujahidin* in Afghanistan and Pakistan might now be being repeated with a new generation of jihadi Islamists in formation in Maluku, Sulawesi and Mindanao and, it appears, in Iraq and Afghanistan.

One of the clear lessons to emerge in the wake of the Bali bombing is the importance of international cooperation. This is seen at a number of levels. The remarkable achievements of the Polri–AFP post-bombing investigations in Bali point to the value of cooperation between police forces and investigators in the region. It was immediately clear that the memorandum of understanding signed by Polri commissioner Da'i Bachtiar and the AFP commissioner some months before the October 2002 attack was of great value. The achievements also highlighted the importance of good personal relationships between professionals. Who knows how differently things might have ended up if Pastika had not been assigned to the investigation and if he and Mick Keelty had not struck up a friendship nine years earlier when Pastika had participated in a training program in Canberra? Similarly, it was clear that Graham Ashton's Indonesian linguistic and cultural knowledge made a significant contribution to ensuring the success of the joint investigation.

At another level, the arrest of Hambali in central Thailand served as a timely reminder that national borders can in no way serve to contain the problem of jihadi terrorism and that cooperation rather than denial is in everybody's best interests. This lesson was reinforced in late April 2004 when attacks on police and military posts in the southern provinces alerted the Thai government to the fact that JI is possibly making inroads into transforming a long-running ethno-nationalist conflict into a global jihadi conflict.

Clearly Indonesian agencies will need to work effectively with their counterparts in Singapore, Malaysia, the Philippines, Thailand

and beyond if the good work begun with JI is to be brought to a successful conclusion. For this reason it is very significant that the Transnational Crime Centre, based at the national police headquarters in Jakarta, together with the Jakarta Centre for Law Enforcement Cooperation, located at the national police academy in Semarang, Central Java, were opened with Australian assistance in early July 2004. Australia made a major contribution to the Transnational Crime Centre as part of its A$10 million Counter Terrorism Capacity Building Initiative for Indonesia, and further committed to giving A$38 million in funding over the next five years to the Centre for Law Enforcement Cooperation (having already contributed A$20.4 million as co-chair of this centre), which will provide three-week counter-terrorism training courses to police from 21 nations in the region.

We also need to recognise that in this first decade of the new century Huntington's thesis looks sadly like becoming a self-fulfilling prophecy. The rapid rise in anti-American sentiment across the Muslim world threatens to persuade many ordinary Muslims that the radical Islamists are correct when they allege that the United States and its western allies have declared war on Islam. Recent findings by the Pew Global Attitudes Project, based on interviews with 16,000 people around the globe, point to to an alarming trend:

> [T]he bottom has fallen out of support for America in most of the Muslim world. Negative views of the U.S. among Muslims, which had been largely limited to countries in the Middle East, have spread to Muslim populations in Indonesia and Nigeria. Since last summer, favorable ratings for the U.S. have fallen from 61% to 15% in Indonesia and from 71% to 38% among Muslims in Nigeria.
>
> In the wake of the war, a growing percentage of Muslims see serious threats to Islam. Specifically, majorities in seven of eight Muslim populations surveyed express worries that the U.S. might become a military threat to their countries...
>
> Support for the U.S.-led war on terrorism also has fallen in most Muslim publics. Equally significant, solid majorities in the Palestinian Authority, Indonesia and Jordan and nearly half of those in Morocco and Pakistan say they have at least some confidence in Osama bin Laden to "do the right thing regarding world affairs."

According to other findings of the Pew Global Attitudes Project, while 75 per cent of Indonesians reported having a favourable opinion of the United States in 2000, by 2003 that figure had fallen to 17 per cent. It is difficult to see how sustained success in the struggle against terrorism will be achieved unless this sad state of affairs can be reversed. The United States and its allies urgently need to give attention to how the Muslim world sees them and to seek to engage with the Muslim world in a way that they have never before been able to do. Otherwise, recent advances in the global struggle against jihadi Islamist terrorism threaten to be followed by significant reversals.

Finally, not only is the international climate fraught, but Indonesian society is also fragile and vulnerable, and we need to understand its problems at this difficult point in its transition to democracy. It is important to reflect on what lessons can be learned from the Pakistani experience. Though it is unpopular and unpleasant to talk of radical Islamism ratcheting up its influence over politics, society and culture in incremental, strategic steps, the reality is that a great deal is at stake: to deny the contest is to lose it.

Notes

Chapter 1. The breakthrough

Notes and sources

p. 12. Statement found on Samudra's laptop and apparently written for istimata.com was taken from: Keith Moor, "Murder in Bali (Insight)," *Herald Sun*, 2 October 2003.

p. 13. Quotation from the report written for the ICG by Sidney Jones was taken from: ICG Asia Briefing, *Al-Qaeda in Southeast Asia: The Case of the "Ngruki Network" in Indonesia*, 8 August 2002, p. 1.

pp. 18–19. Quotation from *Time* magazine was taken from: Romesh Ratnesar, "Confessions of an al-Qaeda Terrorist," *Time*, 23 September 2002.

p. 20. Quotation from Graham Ashton was taken from: Keith Moor, "Murder in Bali (Insight)," *Herald Sun*, 2 October 2003.

p. 22. Quotation from Tim Morris was taken from: Keith Moor, "Murder in Bali (Insight)," ibid.

I am indebted to the Joyo News Service email list, with its extensive daily clippings of reporting on Indonesian affairs from around the world, for enabling me to follow investigations of JI and the Bali bombing though the hundreds of articles that have appeared in English-language publications and news services such as Agence France Presse, Antara, the *Age*, the *Sydney Morning Herald*, *Asia Times* (Hong Kong), Associated Press, the *Australian*, the *Australian Financial Review*, *Business Times* (Singapore), the *Courier-Mail* (Brisbane), *Christian Science Monitor*, the *Economist*, *Far Eastern Economic Review*, *Financial Times*, the *Guardian*, the *Herald Sun* (Melbourne), Human Rights Watch, the *Independent* (London), *Inside Indonesia* (Melbourne), *International Herald Tribune*, the *Jakarta Post*, Laksamana.Net (Jakarta), *Los Angeles Times*, *Newsweek*, the *New Yorker*, *New York Times*, RAND Corporation, Reuters, *South China Morning Post* (Hong Kong), *Straits Times* (Singapore), Stratfor, *Tempo* (Jakarta), *Time*, *Van Zorge Report*, the *Wall Street Journal*, the *Washington Post*, and in the transcripts of television and radio programs broadcast by ABC, BBC, CNN and SBS. While an internet search will quickly yield most of this material, I would never have read most of it were it not for Joyo (more than 10,000 pages of material from Joyo were consulted in preparing this book).

Special mention needs to be made here of an unexpectedly helpful source for much of the detail in this chapter. On 2 October 2003 the Melbourne newspaper the *Herald Sun* published a twenty-page investigative report, "Murder in Bali," written by Insight editor Keith Moor. Moor spent two months interviewing people and reading hundreds of pages of court transcripts and other documents.

Further reading
For a comprehensive summary of virtually all that was known, in the public domain, about JI prior to the Bali bombing in October 2002, refer to ICG Asia Briefing, *Al-Qaeda in Southeast Asia: The Case of the "Ngruki Network" in Indonesia*, 8 August 2002. In the twelve months prior to the bombing in Bali a steady stream of information about JI appeared in the media: Sidney Jones's ICG report synthesises all of that material and adds further material from ICG's investigation. Refer also to: ICG Asia Briefing, *Indonesia: Violence and Radical Muslims*, 10 October 2001. Both of these papers can be found at the International Crisis Group website at: <http://www.crisisweb.org/projects/reports.cfm>. In April 2002 the Terrorism Project at the Washington-based Center for Defense Information (CDI) published a very brief report by analyst Reyko Huang entitled "In the Spotlight: Jemaah Islamiah," two months after it had published a slightly longer report by the same analyst entitled "Al-Qaeda in Southeast Asia: Evidence and Response" (<http://www.cdi.org/terrorism/ji-pr.cfm> and <http://www.cdi.org/terrorism/sea-pr.cfm>).

Chapter 2. Understanding radical Islamism

Notes
This chapter represents a substantial development of a paper that was commenced in mid-2002 and was eventually published as: "Making Sense of Jemaah Islamiyah Terrorism and Radical Islamism in Indonesia," in Shahram Akbarzadeh and Samina Yasmeen (eds), *Islam and the West: Reflections from Australia*, UNSW Press, Sydney, 2004.

p. 32. Quotation from Oliver Roy was taken from: Oliver Roy in William Maley (ed), *Fundamentalism Reborn? Afghanistan and the Taliban*, New York University Press, New York, 2001, p. 199.

p. 33. Quotation from Jenny White was taken from: Jenny B. White, *Islamist Mobilization in Turkey: A Study in Vernacular Politics*, University of Washington Press, Seattle, 2002, p. 6.

p. 38. Quotation from Hassan al-Banna was taken from: Malise Ruthven, *Islam in the World*, 2nd edn, Oxford University Press, New York, 2000, p. 309.

p. 43. Quotation from Martin van Bruinessen was taken from: Martin van Bruinessen, "Genealogies of Islamic Radicalism in Indonesia," *South East Asia Research*, 10(2), 2002, pp. 117–54.

Further reading

Since the 11 September 2001 al-Qaeda attacks in the United States a vast range of books purporting to deal with Islam and terrorism has emerged. The following list represents some of the most important and helpful of these recent books, together with a handful of earlier works. No writer is without bias and no writing without weaknesses, but all of the following books make valuable contributions and together serve as an excellent introduction to these issues.

Benjamin, Daniel, and Simon, Steven, *The Age of Sacred Terror: Radical Islam's War against America*, Random House, New York, 2003.

Berman, Paul, *Terror and Liberalism*, W. W. Norton & Company, New York, 2002.

Burke, Jason, *Al-Qaeda: Casting a Shadow of Terror*, I. B. Tauris, London, 2003.

Caleb, Carr, *The Lessons of Terror: A History of Warfare and Civilians*, Random House, New York, 2003.

Esposito, John L., *The Islamic Threat: Myth or Reality?*, Oxford University Press, New York, 1992.

Esposito, John L., *Unholy War: Terror in the Name of Islam*, Oxford University Press, New York, 2002.

Esposito, John L., and Voll, John, *Islam and Democracy*, Oxford University Press, New York, 1996.

Friedman, Thomas L., *Longitudes and Attitudes*, Anchor Books, New York, 2003.

Fuller, Graham E., *The Future of Political Islam*, Palgrave Macmillan, New York, 2003.

Hiro, Dilip, *Holy Wars: The Rise of Islamic Fundamentalism*, Routledge, London, 1989.

Juergensmeyer, Mark, *The New Cold War? Religious Nationalism Confronts the Secular State*, University of California Press, Berkeley, 1994.

Kepel, Gilles (translated by Anthony F. Roberts), *Jihad: The Trail of Political Islam*, The Belknap Press of Harvard University Press, Cambridge, MA, 2002.

Lewis, Bernard, *The Crisis of Islam: Holy War and Unholy Terror*, The Modern Library, New York, 2003.

Maley, William (ed), *Fundamentalism Reborn? Afghanistan and the Taliban*, New York University Press, New York, 2001.

Murphy, Caryle, *Passion for Islam: Shaping the Modern Middle East – the Egyptian Experience*, Scribner, New York, 2002.

Rashid, Ahmed, *Taliban*, I. B. Tauris, London, 2001.

Rashid, Ahmed, *Jihad: The Rise of Militant Islam in Central Asia*, Penguin, New York, 2003.

Ruthven, Malise, *A Fury for God: The Islamist Attack on America*, Granta Books, London and New York, 2002.

Ruthven, Malise, *Islam in the World*, 2nd edn, Oxford University Press, New York, 2000.

Shepard, William, "The Diversity of Islamic Thought in the 20th Century: Towards a Typology," in Suha Taji-Farouki and Basheer Nafi (eds), *Islamic Thought in the Twentieth Century*, I. B. Tauris, London, 2004.

Shepard, William, "Sayyid Qutb's Doctrine of Jahiliyya," *International Journal of Middle East Studies*, 35(4) (November), 2003, pp. 521–45.

Sidahmed, Abdel Salam, and Ehteshami, Anoushiravan (eds), *Islamic Fundamentalism*, Westview Press, Boulder, CO, 1996.

Sivan, Emmanuel, *Radical Islam: Medieval Theology and Modern Politics*, enlarged edn, Yale University Press, New Haven, 1990.

Schwartz, Stephen, *The Two Faces of Islam: The House of Sa'ud from Tradition to Terror*, Doubleday, New York, 2002.

Stern, Jessica, *Terror in the Name of God: Why Religious Militants Kill*, Harper Collins, New York, 2003.

For discussion of Islamic liberalism refer to: Fazlur Rahman, *Islam and Modernity: Transformation of an Intellectual Tradition*, University of Chicago Press, Chicago, 1982; Fazlur Rahman, "Islam: Challenges and Opportunities," in Alford T. Welch and Pierre Cachia (eds), *Islam: Past Influence and Present Challenge*, Edinburgh University Press, Edinburgh, 1979, pp. 315–30; Leonard Binder, *Islamic Liberalism: A Critique of Development Ideologies*, University of Chicago Press, Chicago, 1988, p. 399; and Charles Kurzman, *Liberal Islam*, Oxford University Press, Oxford, 1998.

Chapter 3. Jemaah Islamiyah's struggle

Notes

p. 48. Quotation from the report written for the ICG by Sidney Jones was taken from: ICG Asia Briefing, *Al-Qaeda in Southeast Asia: The Case of the "Ngruki Network" in Indonesia*, 8 August 2002, p. 8.

pp. 49–50. Quotation from Martin van Bruinessen was taken from Martin van Bruinessen, "Genealogies of Islamic Radicalism in Indonesia," *South East Asia Research*, 10(2), 2002, pp. 117–54.

p. 53. Quotation from the report written for the ICG by Sidney Jones was taken from: ICG Asia Briefing, *Al-Qaeda in Southeast Asia: The Case of the "Ngruki Network" in Indonesia*, 8 August 2002, p. 19.

pp. 53–54. Quotation from the ICG report was taken from: ICG Asia Report No. 63, *Jemaah Islamiyah in South East Asia: Damaged but Still Dangerous*, 26 August 2003, p. 5.

Further reading

As has been noted previously, prior to the Bali bombing the most comprehensive scholarly report to tackle the question of Islamist radicalism in Indonesia, and possible links with international terrorism, was that released on 8 August 2002 by the Brussels-based International Crisis Group (ICG): *Al-Qaeda in Southeast Asia: The Case of the "Ngruki Network" in Indonesia*. Two months after the attack in Bali, ICG's representative in Jakarta, Sidney Jones, released a second report on 11 December 2002, *Indonesia Backgrounder: How the Jemaah Islamiyah Terrorist Network Operates*. Then on 26 August 2003, two weeks after the Marriott bombing, ICG published a third comprehensive report on Jemaah Islamiyah entitled *Jemaah Islamiyah in South East Asia: Damaged but Still Dangerous*. This report makes extensive use of interrogation depositions by JI members detained following the Bali bombing to construct a detailed picture of how al-Qaeda-linked terrorist training camps functioned in Pakistan and the Philippines and how JI developed out of cohorts of Southeast Asian *mujahidin* who studied and taught in these camps after fighting in Afghanistan in the late 1980s. The discussion in this chapter draws extensively on the three ICG reports. Careful to avoid casual speculation and, especially in the case of the second report, oriented towards the assembling of data rather than attempting broad-ranging analysis, the reports are rich in detail and provide an unprecedented insight into militant Islamism in Indonesia. Copies of these ICG reports can be downloaded from: <http://www.crisisweb.org/projects/reports.cfm>.

For a comprehensive study of Laskar Jihad see: Robert Hefner, "Civic Pluralism Denied? The New Media and Jihadi Violence in Indonesia," in Dale F. Eickelman and Jon W. Anderson (eds), *New Media in the Muslim World: The Emerging Public Sphere*, Indiana University Press, Bloomington, 2003, pp. 158–79. More global in scope and valuable in its mapping of the influence of Wahhabi and radical Islamist schools of thought is Martin van Bruinessen, "Genealogies of Islamic Radicalism in Post-Suharto Indonesia," *South East Asia Research*, 10(2), 2002, pp. 117–24.

One earlier work that speculated about al-Qaeda connections in Indonesia is Rohan Gunaratna, *Inside al-Qaeda: Global Network of Terror*, C. Hurst & Co., London, 2002. Gunaratna devotes one chapter out of five to dealing with al-Qaeda in Asia ("Asia: al-Qaeda's New Theatre"), almost half of which is concerned with Southeast Asia. Much of what Gunaratna has to say about Indonesia, however, is very general in nature and that which is more specific has been superseded by the ICG reports. Much richer in content about JI and Indonesia is Zachary Abuza, *Militant Islam in Southeast Asia: Crucible of Terror*, Lynne Reiner Publishers, Boulder, CO, 2003. This book, the result of extensive research across the region, devotes one of its six chapters to tracing the development of Jemaah Islamiyah. Unfortunately, it appears that this first edition was rushed to press with undue haste, for the information-packed text is riddled with numerous errors and the analysis does not reflect an intimate understanding of Indonesian society of the kind evident in the writing of Hefner and van Bruinessen.

A valuable recent addition to writing in this area is: Maria Ressa, *Seeds of Terror: An Eyewitness Account of al-Qaeda's Newest Center of Operations in Southeast Asia*, Free Press, New York, 2003. Ressa's book is especially valuable for its coverage of al-Qaeda and JI operations in the Philippines and for its accessible and engaging style.

Chapter 4. The political struggle

Note

p. 65. Quotation from MMI's Yogyakarta Charter is my translation of an excerpt from MMI's *Piagam Yogyakarta* document.

Further reading

Barton, Greg, *Abdurrahman Wahid, Indonesian President, Muslim Democrat: A View from the Inside*, UNSW Press and University of Hawai'i Press, Sydney and Honolulu, 2002.

Barton, Greg and Fealy, Greg (eds), *Nahdlatul Ulama: Traditional Islam and Modernity in Indonesia*, Monash Asia Institute, Clayton, 1996.

Boland, B. J., *The Struggle of Islam in Modern Indonesia*, Martinus Nijhoff, The Hague, 1971.

Diederich, Mathias, "A Closer Look at Dakwah and Politics in Indonesia: The Partai Keadilan," *Archipel*, 64, 2002, pp. 101–15.

Eliraz, Giora, *Islam in Indonesia: Modernism, Radicalism, and the Middle East Dimension*, Sussex Academic Press, Brighton, 2004.

Fealy, Greg, "Rowing in a Typhoon: Nahdlatul Ulama and the Decline of Constitutional Democracy," in David Bourchier and John Legge (eds), *Indonesian Democracy: 1950s and 1990s*, Monash University, Clayton, 1994, pp. 88–98.

Geertz, Clifford, *The Religion of Java*, Free Press, New York, 1960.

Hefner, Robert W., *Civil Islam: Muslims and Democratization in Indonesia*, Princeton University Press, Princeton, 2000.

Hefner, Robert W. and Horvatich, Patricia (eds), *Islam in an Era of Nation States: Politics and Religious Revival in Muslim Southeast Asia*, University of Hawai'i Press, Honolulu, 1997.

Hooker, M. B., *Indonesian Islam: Social Change through Contemporary Fatwa*, Allen & Unwin, Sydney, 2003.

Kingsbury, D., Budiman, A. and Chauvel, R. (eds), *Political Islam in Indonesia*, Monash University Press, Melbourne, 2004.

Lindsey, T. and Dick, H. (eds), *Corruption in Asia: Rethinking the Good Governance Paradigm*, Federation Press, Sydney, 2002.

Nakamura, Mitsuo, *The Crescent Arises over the Banyan Tree: A Study of the Muhammadiyah Movement in a Central Javanese Town*, Gadjah Mada University Press, Yogyakarta, 1983.

Noer, Deliar, *The Modernist Muslim Movement in Indonesia*, Oxford University Press, Singapore, 1973.

Ramage, Douglas E., *Politics in Indonesia: Democracy, Islam and the Ideology of Tolerance*, Routledge, London, 1995.

van Bruinessen, Martin. "Islamic State or State Islam? Fifty Years of State–Islam Relations in Indonesia," in Ingrid Wessel (ed), *Indonesien am Ende des 20*, Abera-Verlag, 1996, Jahrhunderts, Hamburg, pp. 19–34.

Chapter 5. Responding to radical Islamism

Notes

p. 82. Quotations from Huntington were taken from: Samuel P. Huntington, *The Clash of Civilizations and the Remaking of the World Order*, Simon & Schuster, New York, 1996, pp. 209 and 217–18.

pp. 83–84. Quotation from Berman was taken from: Paul Berman, *Terror and Liberalism*, W. W. Norton & Company, New York, 2002, p. 77.

p. 88. Quotation from the Pew survey was taken from the introduction and summary of The Pew Global Attitudes Project, *Views of a Changing World 2003*, at: <http://people-press.org/reports/display.php3?ReportID=185>. The full report is at: <http://people-press.org/reports/pdf/185.pdf>.

People mentioned in the text

The following information is assembled from reliable sources, including especially the ICG reports, but some details remain disputed and uncertain. For consistency, names (along with common aliases) are listed under notional "surnames" even though this is an alien concept for many Indonesian names (and, indeed, many Indonesians have only one name). I have generally followed the ICG reports and the conventions of *Tempo* magazine when spelling Indonesian names. Although they are not used in the text I have attempted to list common aliases here. There are often many variant spellings of names and this list is not exhaustive.

Abbas, Mohammed Nasir bin (alias Chairudin)
Deputy head of Mantiqi III (covering Mindanao, Sabah and Sulawesi and specialising in training), an Afghan alumni whose sister married Mukhlas. Arrested in April 2003.

Abdalla, Ulil Abshar
Leading young progressive Islamic intellectual, founder of Liberal Islamic Network (JIL), graduate of an NU *pesantren*.

Abduh, Muhammad (b. 1849 in Egypt – d. 1905)
Islamic reformist scholar and seminal contributor to Islamic Modernism.

al-Banna, Hassan (b. 1906 in Egypt – assassinated 1949)
Egyptian Islamist activist. He founded the Muslim Brotherhood (Jamaat al-Islam al-Ikhwan al-Muslimun) in 1928 to strengthen Muslim society in the wake of the collapse of the Ottoman caliphate and the onslaught of corrupting western civilisation, with the eventual aim of creating an Islamic state. Inspired Sayyid Qutb to systematise his vision and extend the program of the Muslim Brotherhood.

al-Faruq, Omar (b. 1971 in Kuwait)
Afghan alumni, alleged coordinator of al-Qaeda operations in Southeast Asia. Moved to Mindanao in 1995 and to Indonesia in 1998. Arrested May 2003. Details of alleged confession published in *Time* on 9 September 2003.

PEOPLE MENTIONED IN THE TEXT

al-Furkan, Abu
A JI member alleged (by Omar al-Faruq) to have been dispatched by Ba'asyir to direct an attack on the US Embassy in Kuala Lumpur.

al-Gaza'iri, al-Mughira
Camp leader of al-Qaeda training base in Khaldan, Afghanistan.

al-Ghozi, Fathur Rahman (b. circa 1972 in Madiun, East Java – shot dead in October 2003)
Graduated from Ba'asyir's Pondok Ngruki *pesantren* in 1989. As a star Afghan alumni, was sent to establish a JI training base in Mindanao in 1996. Arrested in Manila in January 2002, he walked out of jail in July 2003 and was shot dead in Mindanao three months later.

al-Khattab, Ibin
Al-Qaeda-linked Chechen leader said to be in contact with JI leaders such as Fathur Rahman al-Ghozi and Omar al-Faruq.

al-Wahhab, Muhammad ibn Abd (b. 1703 in the Najd, Arabia – d. 1792)
Islamic scholar and founder of the strict Salafy (Wahhabi) reformist movement that opposed Sufism and mystical traditionalism and still dominates Saudi Arabian society.

Amrozi (b. 1963 in Tenggulun, Lamongan, East Java)
Younger brother of Mukhlas (whom he studied with at the Lukmanul Hakiem *pesantren* in Johor, Malaysia) and older brother of Ali Imron; all three brothers were prosecuted for their roles in the Bali bombing. Arrested November 2002, tried in Denpasar in July 2003.

Ansori, Abdullah (alias Abu Fatih, alias Ibnu Thoyib) (b. Pacitan, East Java)
Brother of Ngruki teacher Abdul Rochim, he joined Sungkar and Ba'asyir in Malaysia in 1986, where he helped recruit *mujahidin* for Afghanistan; he later trained in Mindanao.

Armitage, Richard (b. 1945)
US Deputy Secretary of State in the administration of President George W. Bush, he was a former US Navy Seal who served in Vietnam, and a former Assistant Secretary of Defense.

Ashton, Graham (b. 1962)
A highly respected career AFP officer. Attached for three years to the Australian embassy in Jakarta in the 1990s as a liaison officer, he is fluent in Indonesian. Put in charge of the AFP investigation in Bali shortly after the 12 October 2002 bombing.

Awwas, Irfan (alias Irfan Suryahardy) (b. 1960 in East Lombok)
Graduate of the Gontor *pesantren*, he gained prominence for his leadership of BKPM in Yogyakarta in the early 1980s, when he became close friends with Agus Dwikarna, and notoriety for his fiery reporting on the Sungkar–Ba'asyir trial. Consequently spent 1984–93 in prison after being convicted of subversion. Brother of Fihirudin, Head of the Executive Committee of MMI.

Aziz, Abdul (see Samudra, Imam)

Azzam, Abdullah
Close associate of Osama bin Laden in Afghanistan and Pakistan through whom some JI leaders, such as Abdullah Ansori, met bin Laden.

Ba'asyir, Abu Bakar (b. 1938 in Jombang, East Java)
Like many others of Hadrami (Yemeni) descent he was active in al-Irsyad. Together with Abdullah Sungkar he founded Pondok Ngruki *pesantren* in Solo, Central Java, in 1973, and together with Sungkar was arrested in 1978 and released in 1982. Fled to Malaysia in 1985, returned to Indonesia in 1998 and established MMI in August 2000. Arrested October 2002, tried in Jakarta in August 2003 and sentenced to four years in jail. Released on appeal after serving an eighteen-month sentence for immigration offences, he was re-arrested as he left the prison compound on 29 April 2004. The Constitutional Court's 23 July announcement that it had voted to rule invalid the charging of the Bali bombers under Law No. 16/2003 on the grounds that the Indonesian constitution proscribed retrospective application of legislation (except in the case of "extraordinary crime") raised the possibility that Ba'asyir might again be released.

Bachtiar, Da'i
National chief of police in Indonesia. Together with Mick Keelty he was honoured by President Megawati for outstanding cooperation between Polri and the AFP in the Bali bombing investigation.

Bafana, Faiz Abu Bakar (b. 1962 in Singapore)
An Afghan alumni, he is the older brother of Fathi Abu Bakar Bafana. Grew up in Jakarta and became involved with Sungkar, Ba'asyir and the Ngruki circle in 1987. Helped plan attacks in Manila, Singapore and Indonesia with Fathur Rahman al-Ghozi and Hambali. Gave damning evidence against Ba'asyir in court in Singapore. Arrested January 2002.

Bafana, Fathi Abu Bakar
Afghan alumni, member of JI in Malaysia and younger brother of Faiz Abu Bakar Bafana.

PEOPLE MENTIONED IN THE TEXT

Baraja, Abdul Qadir
Member of the executive leadership of MMI in charge of fatwa.

Berman, Paul
American social commentator and writer, author of *Terror and Liberalism*.

Besar, Umar (see Ghani, Abdul)

Dahdah, Abu
Alleged leader of al-Qaeda in Spain; has visited Indonesia and worked with JI.

Dul Matin (b. 1970 in Petarukan, Pemalang, Central Java)
Afghan alumni, frequent visitor to Ngruki, expert in bomb construction, apparently involved in all of JI's major bombings including Bali. At the time of writing he has eluded capture.

Dwikarna, Agus (b. 1964 in Makassar, South Sulawesi)
Active in the mainstream Islamic student association HMI–MPO in Yogyakarta in the early 1980s, when he became a close friend of Irfan Awwas, and then in PAN. Appointed general secretary of MMI, head of Laskar Jundullah and KOMPAK. Arrested March 2002 at Manila airport, apparently through a set-up.

Fatih, Abu (see Ansori, Abdullah)

Fihirudin (see Jibril, Abu)

Ghani, Abdul (alias Umar Besar – "Big Umar")
Involved in the Christmas Eve 2000 church bombings and the Bali bombing. Arrested April 2003.

Gufron, Ali (see Mukhlas)

Hambali (alias Riduan Isomuddin) (b. 1964 in Cianjur, West Java)
Afghan alumni whose parents were active in the Darul Islam struggle. Became close to Abdullah Sungkar while in Afghanistan in the late 1980s. Head of JI in Malaysia and Singapore (Mantiqi I) but also a senior JI leader with broader planning responsibilities for field operations. As mastermind of Bali bombing, he has close ties to al-Qaeda. Arrested in Thailand in August 2003; currently detained in US custody.

Haz, Hamzah
NU leader and chairman of PPP. Served as Megawati's vice-president from July 2001 to October 2004. Outspoken defender of Jafar Umar Thalib and Abu Bakar Ba'asyir.

Hendropriyono, A. M.
TNI general with long association with military intelligence. Head of BIN and senior cabinet minister under the Megawati administration. In 1989 he led an attack on a Darul Islam/JI community in Way Jepara, Lampung, South Sulawesi, founded by Abdullah Sungkar, that resulted in the deaths of more than 100 people. In late May and early June 2004, in response to reports that he had lobbied for Sidney Jones to be expelled from Indonesia, he argued that the ICG reports "were not all true," and explained that "actions should be taken against those... who damage the country's image." Some analysts have speculated that Hendropriyono was annoyed at the fact that Polri, and not BIN, was receiving all the credit for successes against JI.

Hispan (a contraction of Haji Ismail Pranoto)
Leader of Darul Islam/NII to whom Abdullah Sungkar and Abu Bakar Ba'asyir allegedly swore allegiance in 1976, for which reason they were arrested in 1978.

Huntington, Samuel
Harvard University political science professor whose much talked-about 1993 essay in *Foreign Affairs*, "The Clash of Civilizations?" (borrowing the language of Bernard Lewis), became the basis of the 1996 book *The Clash of Civilizations and the Remaking of World Order*, which controversially predicted a clash between the west and the Muslim world.

Husin, Dr Azahari (b. 1957 in Malaysia)
Afghan alumni, Mindanao alumni, British-trained engineer and former lecturer at University Teknologi Malaysia in Johor. Board member of Lukmanul Hakiem *pesantren*. JI's leading expert on, and instructor in, bomb-making; involved in Christmas Eve 2000 and Bali bombings. At the time of writing he has eluded capture.

Idris
One of the JI team directly involved with the bombing in Bali, he was responsible for accommodation and other logistical and financial arrangements in Denpasar ahead of the bombing. Arrested in June 2003.

Imron, Ali
Younger brother of Amrozi and Mukhlas. Studied in Pakistan in 1995, and in Ngruki for several months. Apart from his year in Pakistan, lived in Malaysia with Mukhlas between 1990 and 1998 studying at Lukmanul Hakiem *pesantren* in Johor. Reportedly drove the Mitsubishi L300 van used in the bombing from the family home in Lamongan, East Java to Denpasar, Bali. Arrested in January 2003 and tried in Denpasar in July 2003.

PEOPLE MENTIONED IN THE TEXT

Iqbal (alias Armasan, alias Lacong) (b. 1980 in Sukamana, Banten, West Java – d. 12 October 2002)
The JI suicide bomber who walked into Paddy's Bar on the evening of 12 October 2002 and detonated his explosive vest seconds before Jimi detonated his car bomb, driving the dozens of patrons of Paddy's not killed by his bomb out into Jalan Legian, where they were hit with the blast from Jimi's massive charge. Iqbal was apparently a member of Imam Samudra's cell.

Isomuddin, Riduan (see Hambali)

Jibril, Abu (alias Fihirudin) (b. East Lombok)
Brother of Irfan Awwas, he achieved prominence as a fiery *muballigh* (lay preacher) in Yogyakarta in the early 1980s. Joined Sungkar and Ba'asyir in exile in Malaysia in 1985. Member of the MMI national executive. Arrested June 2001.

Jimi (d. 12 October 2002)
The JI suicide bomber who drove the explosive-packed Mitsubishi L300 to the front of the Sari Club and detonated the bomb.

Jones, Sidney (b. 1952)
American researcher in charge, since 2002, of the Indonesian program of the International Crisis Group (ICG), the Brussels-based international research institute led by former Australian foreign minister Gareth Evans. Prior to this she worked in the New York office of Human Rights Watch for fourteen years, and from 1977 to 1982 she worked in the Jakarta office of the Ford Foundation, during which time she also undertook postgraduate research on Islam. In late May 2004 it was announced that the Indonesian government would not be renewing Jones's work permit, effectively expelling her from Indonesia, apparently because the ICG's reporting, not just on JI but also on conflict in Aceh and Papua, had upset BIN chief, and influential cabinet minister, General A. M. Hendropriyono.

Kalla, Yusuf
Successful Bugis businessman and Golkar politician from South Sulawesi. Trade and industry minister in the Wahid cabinet and coordinating minister for people's welfare in the Megawati cabinet. Helped broker a vital peace accord in Maluku in February 2002. In May 2004 Yudhoyono announced Kalla as his running mate in the presidential election.

Kartosuwirjo, Sekarmadji Maridjan
Muhammadiyah-educated, leader of the Darul Islam movement in West Java in the 1950s, mentor of Kahar Muzzakar and later a heroically inspirational figure for Sungkar and Ba'asyir and others in JI. In 1948 he

established TII and in August 1949 proclaimed the Islamic State of Indonesia (NII) in the Darul Islam (abode of Islam) areas of West Java under his control. Arrested in 1962.

Kecil, Umar ("little Umar" – see Patek, Umar)

Keelty, Mick (b. 1954 –)
Dubbed "the quiet achiever," AFP Commissioner Mick Keelty's gentle approach to regional cooperation proved invaluable in the wake of the Bali bombing. He enjoyed a good relationship with Indonesian police chief Da'i Bachtiar and formed a firm friendship with Pastika since the latter had participated in a Serious Crime course in Canberra in 1993, all of which helped make possible the forming of a joint Polri–AFP investigation within a week of the bombing. In June 2003 President Megawati awarded Keelty Polri's highest honour in recognition of outstanding cooperation between Polri and the AFP in the investigation.

Laden, Osama bin (b. 1957 in Saudi Arabia)
Born into a large family with humble Hadrami (Yemeni) origins but grown wealthy through a highly successful construction business, bin Laden was drawn to dissident Islamist circles. In 1979 he left Saudi Arabia to join the struggle against the Soviets in Afghanistan, and there he established his Maktab al-Khidmat (MAK) service base to equip and train foreign *mujahidin*, including, beginning in the mid-1980s, hundreds of Southeast Asians. The *mujahidin* fought the Soviets with the help of the CIA but after the Soviet withdrawal in 1989 many, including bin Laden, began to turn their attention to the Saudi regime and its ally America. Bin Laden returned to Saudi Arabia but was expelled in 1991 for dissident activities; he then lived in Sudan for five years but pressure from America saw him expelled and he fled to Afghanistan where, as leader of what came to be known as al-Qaeda, he helped equip *mujahidin* for a global struggle.

Ma'arif, Dr Ahmad Syafi'i (b. circa 1941 in Central Java)
Educated in Muhammadiyah schools, Ma'arif obtained a PhD from Chicago University at around the same time as Nurcholish Madjid and Amien Rais. In 1998 he took over from Amien Rais to become interim chairman of Muhammadiyah and in 2000 he was elected to a five-year term as leader of this 30-million-strong modernist organisation. Compared with Amien Rais and several other senior leaders, he is regarded as a progressive intellectual critical of radical Islamism.

Madjid, Nurcholish (b. 1941 in Jombang, East Java)
A graduate of his father's *madrasah*, Madjid went on to study at the influential Pesantren Modern in Gontor before undertaking PhD studies at the

University of Chicago under Fazlur Rahman. Since returning to Indonesia he has channelled his efforts in progressive religious education through his foundation Paramadina. A prolific writer, with Abdurrahman Wahid he has helped establish liberal Islamic thought in Indonesia.

Mahendra, Yusril Izha
Chairman of PBB, former professor of law and former speech-writer for Soeharto, and minister for justice under both Wahid and Megawati. Mahendra, who makes no secret of his radical Islamist convictions and has been outspoken in his defence of Abu Bakar Ba'asyir, has assured MMI that he will continue to work to change Indonesia's law to incrementally implement the Shariah.

Masduki, Ajengan
Darul Islam/NII leader previously close to Abdullah Sungkar. It is thought that Sungkar's falling out with Masduki in 1992–93 precipitated the formation of JI.

Maududi, Abu'l Ala (b. 1903 in Hyderabad, India – d. 1979 in Pakistan)
One of the twentieth century's most influential Islamic writers, in large part because of his appealing systematisation of ideas and his ability to communicate in plain language. Maududi was largely self-taught and for many years worked as a professional journalist. In 1940 he founded the organisation-cum-political-party Jamaat-i-Islami and served as its *amir* for the next three decades. His ideas became increasingly radical and he pioneered the application of the Marxist revolutionary idea of a vanguard to the Islamist struggle, which was later further developed by Sayyid Qutb; nevertheless, he remained committed to using political means. His writings have been very influential in modernist circles in Indonesia.

Morris, Tim
The AFP's director of counter-terrorism, who headed up the Australia-based end of the Bali bombing investigation.

Mukhlas (alias Ali Gufron) (b. 1960 in Tenggulun, Lamongan, East Java –)
Afghan alumni, older brother of Amrozi and Ali Imron. Graduated from Ngruki in 1982, founded Lukmanul Hakiem *pesantren* in Johor, Malaysia in 1991, and is said to have replaced Hambali as head of JI operations in Malaysia and Singapore (Mantiqi I). He married the sister of Nasir bin Abbas. Played a lead role in the Bali bombing.

Murdani, Benny
A career officer close to Soeharto and protégé of Ali Murtopo. Born into a

Catholic family in Java, Murdani rose to the position of commander of ABRI until his frank advice to Soeharto about the errant ways of his children saw him promoted to minister of defence in 1988. A controversial figure reviled by many Muslims for his part in the harsh repression of Islamist activists by military intelligence officers and Special Forces troops, most notably in the Tandjung Priok massacre of 1984.

Murtopo, Ali
A confidant of Soeharto, General Ali Murtopo was minister of information and head of Opsus in the 1970s and 1980s. In the 1980s he managed to convince a number of Darul Islam's old warriors to come out into the open and join him in the fight against "the Communists" as Komando Jihad.

Muzadi, Hasyim
Replaced Abdurrahman Wahid as chairman of NU in 1999, and said to be close to Megawati's powerful husband, Taufiq Kiemas. In May 2004 he was selected to become Megawati's running mate.

Muzakkar, Kahar (also spelt Qahhar Mudzakkar) (b. in Lulu, South Sulawesi)
Muhammadiyah-educated, one-time bodyguard of Sukarno and well-regarded nationalist. He was active in Hizbullah, then leader of militia groups that fought the Dutch during the Revolution but then rebelled in 1949 when they were not accepted into Indonesia's post-independence army. Joined forces with Kartosuwirjo in January 1952 when he was offered the post of commander of TII in South Sulawesi as an expression of solidarity with Darul Islam in West Java. In 1953 he declared Sulawesi to be part of NRII and for the next decade fought to establish an Islamic state. Arrested in 1965.

Natsir, Mohammad (b. 1908 in West Sumatra – d. 1993)
Leader of MIAI during the Japanese occupation, then of Masyumi in the 1940s and 1950s. A member of Persis, and a prominent nationalist who served as prime minister between 1950 and 1951. Later fell out with Sukarno and led the PRRI revolt in West Sumatra in 1958 only to see his beloved Masyumi banned in January 1960. In 1967, disappointed with Soeharto's control over Masyumi's successor, Parmusi, and becoming steadily more radical, he turned to civil-sphere activism and established DDII.

Pastika, General I Made Mangku (b. 1951 in Bali)
One of Indonesia's most respected police officers. Served as the liaison between the Indonesian government, the UN administration and the UN Mission in East Timor in 1999, and investigated the deaths of three UN

workers in Atambua. Was then assigned to Papua where he dealt with a hostage crisis and investigated the death in TNI custody of Papua activist leader Theys Eluay and the shooting murder of one Indonesian and two American teachers in an ambush near the Freeport copper mine in Timika. Pastika was appointed to head the Bali investigation after the bombing; in May 2003 the two-star general was transferred to the one-star position of chief of police in Bali.

Patek, Umar (alias Umar Kecil – "Little Umar")
One of the JI bombers involved in the Bali operation. At the time of writing he has eluded capture.

Qatada, Abu (b. circa 1960)
The alleged leader, or at least spiritual adviser, of al-Qaeda in Europe. Detained by MI5 in October 2002, the Palestinian radical Islamist is wanted on terrorism charges in Jordan. He is reportedly a friend of Sheikh Omran in Melbourne and Bilal Khazal in Sydney and has been linked with Abu Bakar Ba'asyir via an al-Qaeda cell in Spain.

Qutb, Muhammad
Younger brother of Sayyid Qutb. Moved to Saudi Arabia after the execution of his brother in 1966, where he taught Islamic studies, expounded the ideas of Sayyid Qutb and established a reputation in his own right.

Qutb, Sayyid (b. 1906 in rural Upper Egypt, arrested 1954, executed 1966)
Enormously influential as the seminal thinker behind jihadi Islamism. Worked as an official in the Egyptian ministry of education, travelled to the US in November 1948 for two years of study, before returning to Egypt in August 1950 to devote himself to the Muslim Brotherhood. Convinced that only a purified Islam could save the world, he wrote an innovative, stirring, 30-part commentary on the Qur'an which began to appear in 1952. He continued in prison where his writing became increasingly dark, to the point were he became convinced that the whole world, including virtually all Muslim communities, were lost in wretched spiritual ignorance (*jahiliah*). He combined the ideas of Maududi and radical Marxist ideas of revolution with al-Banna's Islamist reformism and Ibn Taymiyya's fourteenth-century Puritanism and declared that a small vanguard of *mujahidin* must dedicate themselves to the long struggle to form a pure Islamic society.

Rahman, Fazlur (b. 1919 in Pakistan – d. 1988)
The definitive late-twentieth-century liberal Islamic intellectual. Studied at

Punjab University and Oxford and taught in England and Canada before returning to Pakistan in 1961 where he was asked to lead the progressive Central Institute of Islamic Research in Karachi. In the face of mounting opposition he was forced to flee Pakistan in 1968 for the University of Chicago, where he taught until his death. He was enormously influential around the world, but especially in Indonesia where Nurcholish Madjid and other students further developed his vision of combining the best of classical, traditional Islamic scholarship, Islamic modernism and western learning to create a dynamic synthesis he dubbed Islamic neo-modernism. The Rahman-inspired liberalism of Nurcholish Madjid, Abdurrahman Wahid and Ulil Abshar Abdalla is an enduring source of irritation to radical Islamists in Indonesia today.

Rahman, Sheikh Umar Abdul

Former leader of Gama Islami jailed for his part in the 1993 attack on the World Trade Center.

Rais, Dr Amien (b. 1944 in Solo, Central Java)

Appointed to a five-year term as chairman of the 30-million-strong modernist mass organisation Muhammadiyah, he stepped down in 1998 (handing the reins to Syafi'i Ma'arif) to take up the leadership of PAN. Received a PhD in political science from the University of Chicago but, unlike Nurcholish Madjid and Syafi'i Ma'arif, was not supervised by, and did not take on board, the liberal ideas of Chicago's Fazlur Rahman. Played a key role in assembling the temporary Central Axis coalition of Islamic parties that out-manoeuvred Megawati and PDIP to get Abdurrahman Wahid elected president in 1999, only then to campaign for his removal (and later call for the removal of Megawati). His outspokenness and penchant for switching from Islamist firebrand to moderate Muslim statesman and back again has cost him credibility in many circles.

Rida, Rashid (b. 1865 in Lebanon – d. 1935)

Theorist who influenced Islamic modernism in Indonesia from the founding of Muhammadiyah in 1912 up until the present, especially among Islamists. Moved to Egypt in 1897 to join Muhammad Abduh and went on to become his most influential disciple, publishing the monthly modernist journal *al-Manar* (the *Lighthouse*) from 1898 until 1935. Rida's interpretation of Islamic modernism became increasingly Islamist and deviated from Abduh's original emphasis on tolerance and cultural change.

Roy, Oliver

Influential French scholar and writer who has written extensively about political Islam and Islam in Central Asia, Afghanistan and Pakistan.

PEOPLE MENTIONED IN THE TEXT

Rusdan, Abu (also known as Thoriqudin) (b. in Kudus, Central Java)
An Afghan alumni, Rusdan is the son of a jailed Darul Islam–Komando Jihad activist. He spent much time with Sungkar and Ba'asyir while they were in exile in Malaysia and is said to have replaced Ba'asyir as *amir* of JI following Ba'asyir's arrest in October 2002. Arrested in April 2003.

Rushdi, Usama
A leader of Gama Islami, the radical breakaway faction of the Muslim Brotherhood, who became close to Abdullah Sungkar and Abu Bakar Ba'asyir.

Samudra, Imam (alias Abdul Aziz)
Born in Serang, Banten, West Java into a staunch Persis family, gained prominence as a radical Islamist activist, moved to Malaysia in 1990 to join Sungkar and Ba'asyir. Highly intelligent, Samudra is regarded as the field commander of the Bali bombing. Arrested in November 2002.

Sayyaf, Abdul Rasul
Close associate of Osama bin Laden, Afghan *mujahidin* commander, and commander of Camp Saddah, the al-Qaeda training camp in Khumran Agency, Parachinar, Pakistan. The Philippines terrorist group Abu Sayyaf is said to be named after him.

Sukarnoputri, Megawati
The daughter of Sukarno, Megawati shot to prominence after Soeharto had her deposed from the leadership of PDI and then sent troops to storm her supporters in the PDI headquarters in Central Jakarta in July 1996. These events established her as a figurehead of the reformist movement after the fall of Soeharto in May 1998. In October she missed out on being voted president after a temporary alliance of Islamic parties secured victory for Abdurrahman Wahid, becoming vice-president instead. In July 2001 she replaced the beleaguered Wahid as president when the Consultative Assembly voted him out of office.

Sungkar, Abdullah (b. 1937 in Solo – d. 1999)
Close friend of Abu Bakar Ba'asyir, together with whom he founded Pesantren al-Mukmin (Pondok Ngruki) in Ngruki, Solo, in 1973. Jailed together with Ba'asyir in 1978, released in 1983, fled to exile with Ba'asyir in Malaysia in 1985. Sungkar and Ba'asyir established JI while in Malaysia in the mid-1990s.

Suryahardy, Irfan (see Awwas, Irfan)

Taymiyya, Ibn (b. 1263 in Harran – d. 1328 in Cairo)
The writings of Taymiyya, a jurist from the pietistic Hanbali school, are

popular among Wahhabi Salafy scholars and Islamists generally, in part because of his fiery denouncement of the irreligiosity of the invading Mongols, but liberals such as Nurcholish Madjid have also benefited from his insights.

Thalib, Jafar Umar (b. 1961 in Malang)
Afghan alumni, son of a strict Hadrami religious leader. Went to study in Saudi Arabia in 1986 on a scholarship from DDII, then in 1987 went to Afghanistan where he spent two years as a *mujahidin*; he later spent time studying in Yemen and Pakistan. Established a jihadi Islamist *pesantren* on the outskirts of Yogyakarta in 1994; in Solo in February 1998 he founded Forum Komunikasi Ahlus Sunnah wal Jamaah (FKAWJ) and in February 2000 he established the jihadi Islamist militia Laskar Jihad, under the auspices of FKAWJ, to send *mujahidin* to Maluku.

Thoriqudin (see Rusdan, Abu)

van Bruinessen, Martin
Dutch anthropologist and leading expert on Islam and Muslim society in Indonesia.

Wahid, Abdurrahman (b. 1940 in Jombang, East Java)
Son and grandson of NU founders and leaders, he studied in *pesantren* in Java and then at Al-Azhar University in Cairo for two years and at Baghdad University for four years. Served as chairman of NU from 1984 until 1999, when he was elected president. Sacked by the Consultative Assembly in July 2001, he was replaced by Megawati. An outspoken critic of the Soeharto regime and one of Indonesia's leading liberal Islamic intellectuals.

Wahid, Hidayat Nur
Leader of PK and PKS

Wan Mat, Wan Min bin (b. 1960 in Kelantan, Malaysia)
Lecturer at University Teknologi Malaysia in Johor, Joined Sungkar and Ba'asyir's circle in 1993 and became treasurer of JI. Arrested in September 2002.

Warsidi (d. 1989)
A leader of the Darul Islam community established by Abdullah Sungkar in Way Jepara, Lampung, South Sumatra. Killed in the raid by Ali Murtopo's troops in 1989.

Yudhoyono, Susilo Bambang (b. Pacitan, East Java, 1949)
Son of a retired army officer. Though a bookish and quiet child from an early age, Yudhoyono – or SBY as he is popularly known – desired a mili-

tary career and went on to graduate from the National Military Academy in Malang in 1973 at the top of his class. He was commander of Kostrad (Strategic Reserves) Infantry Airborne Battalion 330 from 1974 to 1976, was twice deployed to East Timor (1979–80 and 1986–88) and become a lecturer at the Army Staff and Command School in Bandung in 1989 having earlier earned a masters degree from Webster University in the US. After two years in Bandung he studied at the Command and General Staff College in Fort Leavenworth, Kansas, and later served in Bosnia-Hezegovina with United Nations Peacekeeping Forces (1995–96). He was promoted to Chief of Staff of the Jakarta Regional Command in 1996, then a command post in Sumatra before finally being appointed to the post of the army's Social-Political Assistant, in which position he gained credit for conceptualising military reform. SBY was sworn in to the Wahid cabinet in October 1999 as minister for mines and energy but months later was made coordinating minister for politics and security, in which role he worked on conflict resolution in Papua, Aceh and West Timor. He became one of President Wahid's most trusted ministers and, although sacked at the very end of the Wahid presidency, he went on to serve in the Megawati cabinet in the same role. When he became involved in the formation of the Democratic Party in 2002 few credited him or his party with being likely to secure the presidency after Megawati but his departure from her cabinet in March 2004 saw his popularity soar to remarkable heights.

Zubaydah, Abu
Close associate of Osama bin Laden who helped introduce Omar al-Faruq to al-Qaeda.

Zulkarnaen (true name is Aris Sumarsono) (b. circa 1962)
Afghan alumni. Graduated from Ngruki in 1979. One of the very first Indonesians to go to Sayyaf's Camp Saddah in 1985, and later took charge of the Southeast Asian training program at Camp Saddah.

Glossary of terms and abbreviations

ABRI: Angkatan Bersenjata Republik Indonesia, the Indonesian Armed Forces

Abu Sayyaf: terrorist group cum criminal gang in Mindanao, linked to al-Qaeda

Afghan alumni: *mujahidin* who trained and fought in Afghanistan/Pakistan

AFP: Australian Federal Police

al-Ikhwan al-Muslimun: the Muslim Brotherhood

al-Irsyad: an Islamist organisation supported particularly by Indonesian Muslims of Arab descent

al-Qaeda: "the base," a network of networks engaged in jihadi terrorism, wrapped around a small inner core associated with Saudi exile Osama bin Laden, which coalesced in Afghanistan in the late 1990s and achieved notoriety with the 11 September 2001 attacks on America

BAKIN: Badan Koordinasi Intelijens Nasional (National Intelligence Coordinating Body), the precursor to BIN, Indonesia's peak intelligence agency

bayyat: a vow of loyalty, such as is frequently made by disciples to their religious leader; in al-Qaeda and JI, followers pledge to obey the *amir* in all matters except if he acts contrary to God

BIN: Badan Intelijens Nasional (National Intelligence Body), Indonesia's peak intelligence agency, led by Hendropriyono

BKPM: Badan Koordinasi Pemuda Mesjid (Coordinating Body for Mosque Youth)

Camp Abu Bakar: the extensive MILF training camp in Mindanao which provided large-scale training facilities for JI between 1996, when the situation in Afghanistan and in Camp Saddah changed, and 2000, when Philippines forces overran the camp

Camp Hudaibiyah: the JI training camp established in 1996 in one corner of Camp Abu Bakar as JI's main, post-Afghanistan, training camp

GLOSSARY

Camp Saddah: the *mujahidin* training camp with close ties to what became al-Qaeda, where most Southeast Asian *mujahidin* trained, located in the Khumran Agency, Parachinar, Pakistan, on the border with Afghanistan

dakwah: religious missionary endeavours, including proselytising, teaching and strengthening believers in their faith

DDII: Dewan Dakwah Islamiyah Indonesia (Indonesian Council for Islamic Dakwah), radical Islamist NGO founded by Mohammad Natsir in 1967, linked to Rabitat al-Alam al Islami

ETA: the Basque separatist group active in north-western Spain

FKAWJ: Forum Komunikasi Ahlus Sunnah wal Jamaah (Communication Forum of the Followers of the Sunnah and the Community of the Prophet), the jihadi Islamist organisation that established Laskar Jihad

Gama Islami (al-Gama'at al-Islamiyah): the radical breakaway faction of the Muslim Brotherhood

Golkar: the ruling political vehicle of the Soeharto regime

GPII: Gerakan Pemuda Islam Indonesia (Indonesian Muslim Youth Movement)

Hizb ut-Tahrir al-Islami: the radical Islamist organisation founded in Jordan in 1953, now established in cities like Solo in Indonesia and linked with MMI

Hizbullah: the war-time militia set up during the Japanese occupation by the major Islamic organisations, active during the revolution

ICG: International Crisis Group

ISI: Pakistan Inter-Services Intelligence directorate, which worked with the CIA to sponsor *mujahidin* fighting in Afghanistan in the 1980s

Jakarta Charter: the section of the 1945 constitution discarded before its promulgation, which stated: "it is obligatory for Muslims to carry out the Shariah"

jemaah: community, assembly, congregation

JI (Jemaah Islamiyah): jihadi Islamist Southeast Asian terrorist network established by Abdullah Sungkar and Abu Bakar Ba'asyir in the early 1990s when they broke from Darul Islam; led by *mujahidin* returned from Afghanistan/Pakistan, independent from, but affiliated with, al-Qaeda

jihad: the Arabic word literally means "to struggle" and is often used of "just war" defensive military action, but the Sufis describe military action as being the "lesser jihad" and describe the personal struggle to overcome base instincts as being the "greater jihad"

JIL: Jaringan Islam Liberal, the Liberal Islamic Network comprised of young progressive Islamic intellectuals from NU and Muhammadiyah inspired by Abdurrahman Wahid and Nurcholish Madjid

KISDI: Komiti Indonesia untuk Solidaritas Dunia Islam (Indonesia Committee for Solidarity with the Muslim World)

Komando Jihad: the regrouping of Darul Islam/NII activists flushed out into the open by Ali Murtopo in the late 1970s

KOMPAK: Komite Aksi Penanggulangan Akibat Krisis (Action Committee for Tackling the Consequences of Crisis), the Islamist relief agency established in Java in 1998 by DDII; also produced propaganda videos of Muslim suffering in Maluku to raise funds, recruit *mujahidin* and purchase weapons

Laskar Jihad: jihadi Islamist militia founded in Java in January 2000, sent forces to Maluku, led by Jafar Umar Thalib; not directly linked to JI, but appeared to have the support of elements within TNI

Laskar Jundullah: jihadi Islamist militia founded in South Sulawesi in 2000, sent forces to Poso, previously led by JI's Agus Dwikarna

Laskar Mujahidin: jihadi Islamist militia linked to JI and active in Maluku

Lukmanul Hakiem: the jihadi Islamist *pesantren* in Johor established by Mukhlas in 1991 and closed done by the Malaysian authorities in 2001

madrasah: in Indonesia *madrasah* are generally Islamic day schools with a largely secular curriculum, and many are located inside *pesantren*; in other countries they often have a narrow Islamic curriculum

MAK: Maktab al-Khidmat (Service College)

Maktab al-Khidmat (MAK): the 'College of the Faithful' in Afghanistan run by Osama bin Laden where most Southeast Asians were processed before proceeding to Camp Saddah, and part of the service organisation that evolved into al-Qaeda

Masjumi: the peak modernist Islamic party after NU split away in 1952 to stand as an independent party

MIAI: Majelis Al Islam A'la Indunisiya (Indonesian Islamic Council)

MILF: The Moro Islamic Liberation Front, the jihadi Islamist organisation that split from the more secular MNLF and developed close links with JI through returning *mujahidin*

GLOSSARY

MMA: Muttahida Majlis-e-Amal (United Action Front), the coalition of six Islamist parties, led by the Jamaat-i-Islami, that contested the 2002 general elections in Pakistan

MMI: Majelis Mujahidin Indonesia (Indonesian Mujahidin Council), the radical/jihadi Islamist umbrella group founded in Yogyakarta in August 2000 by Abu Bakar Ba'asyir

MNLF: Moro National Liberation Front

modernism: Islamic modernism is the reformist movement that began in the nineteenth century, and was significantly developed by Muhammad Abduh at the turn of the century, emphasising accommodation with modern science and technology and *ijtihad*, or fresh individual scholarly interpretation of the Qur'an, and the purifying of Islam from the syncretistic accretions of folk religion

muballigh: Islamic preacher, often not one of the *ulama*

Muhammadiyah: Indonesia's 30-million-strong modernist Islamist mass organisation founded in 1912

mujahidin: those engaged in jihad, Muslim fighters

Mujahidin KOMPAK: jihadi Islamist militia founded in 1999 by the Solo branch of KOMPAK, linked to but independent from JI, sent forces to Maluku, and later to Sulawesi, served as an umbrella group for *mujahidin*

Muslim Brotherhood: a reformist Islamist movement started in Egypt by Hassan al-Banna in 1928 and reinvigorated by Sayyid Qutb in the 1950s

neo-modernism: a liberal Islamic movement combining modernist rationalism with traditionalist scholarship and modern western learning first articulated by Fazlur Rahman and developed in Indonesia by Nurcholish Madjid and Abdurrahman Wahid

NII: Negara Islam Indonesia (Islamic State of Indonesia)

NRII: Negara Republik Islam Indonesia (Islamic Republic of Indonesia)

NU: Nahdlatul Ulama (The Arising of the Ulama), Indonesia's mass organisation of traditionalist *ulama* and their *pesantren* communities founded in 1926

Opsus: Operasisi Khusus (Special Operations Service)

Paddy's Bar: crowded bar on Jalan Legian, Kuta, Bali, near Sari Club, where, on 12 October 2002, the first large bomb was detonated by a suicide bomber wearing an explosive vest

PAN: Partai Amanat Nasional (National Mandate Party)

Pancasila: the five-precept formulation that articulates a non-sectarian, theistic-secular doctrine of state for independent Indonesia

Partai Democratic: The Democratic Party headed by Susilo Bambang Yudhoyono

PBB: Partai Bulan Bintang (Crescent Moon and Star Party)

PBR: Partai Bintang Reformasi (Reform Star Party)

PDI: Partai Demokrasi Indonesia (Indonesian Democratic Party)

PDIP: Partai Demokrasi Indonesia Perjuangan (Indonesian Democracy Party of the Struggle)

PDS: Partai Damai Sejahtera (Prosperous Peace Party)

Persis: Persatuan Islam (Islamic Union)

pesantren: Islamic boarding school mostly linked to NU where classical Islamic scholarship, and often Sufism, is taught; generally houses a *madrasah*

PETN: pentaerithrytol tetranitrate

PK: Partai Keadilan (Justice Party)

PKB: Partai Kebangkitan Bangsa (National Awakening Party)

PKS: Partai Keadilan Sejahtera (Prosperous Justice Party)

PNI: Partai Nasional Indonesia (Indonesian Nationalist Party)

Polri: Polisi Republik Indonesia, the Indonesian police force; previously part of the military, then known as ABRI, up until May 1999

Pondok Ngruki: Pesantren al-Mukmin, the jihadi Islamist *pesantren* established by Abdullah Sungkar and Abu Bakar Ba'asyir in 1971, and then in 1973 relocated to the village of Ngruki on the outskirts of Solo, Central Java; many key JI figures have links with Ngruki

PPP: Partai Persatuan Pembangunan (United Development Party)

preman: thugs, gangsters, violent criminals acting in gangs and sometimes drafted into militias

PRRI: Pemerintah Revolusioner Republik Indonesia (Revolutionary Government of the Republic of Indonesia)

Rabitat al-Alam al Islami: Muslim World League, the Saudi Arabian–backed foundation that funded Southeast Asian *mujahidin* in Afghanistan

GLOSSARY

RDX: Royal Demolition eXplosive

Salafy: preferred name of Wahhabi Islamic Puritanism

santri: observant Muslims; originally a term referring specifically to students of *pesantren*

Sari Club: popular thatched-roof nightspot in Jalan Legian, Kuta, Bali, where the vehicle bomb was exploded on 12 October 2002

Shia: the majority form of Islam in Iran and Iraq but a minority element elsewhere, with only around 15 per cent of the world's 1.3 billion Muslims being Shia, the other 85 per cent being Sunni, including virtually all Muslims in Indonesia

Sufism: Islamic mysticism, covering a broad spectrum of belief and practice but united in an emphasis on the heart

Sunni: see: Shia

Tandjung Priok: the impoverished port district of Jakarta and site of an infamous attack on *usrah* Islamist radicals in 1984

TII: Tentara Islam Indonesia (Islamic Army of Indonesia)

TNI: Tentara Nasional Indonesia, the Indonesian armed forces, previously known as ABRI but renamed when the police force was separated from the military in May 1999

traditionalism: Islamic traditionalism, as represented by NU in Indonesia, is not opposed to modernism but seeks to preserve classical Islamic scholarship and certain aspects of folk religion, not least being Sufism and a sense of connection with departed saints

usrah (usroh): cell or study circle, name of an Islamist movement in 1980s

Wahdah Islamiyah: the Darul Islam–inspired jihadi Islamist South Sulawesi group that has loose ties to JI

Wahhabi: Islamic Puritan movement, also called Salafy, originating from Arabia and the eighteenth-century reformist scholar ibn Abd al-Wahhab; it defines the parameters of state religion in Saudi Arabia

Acknowledgements

I am grateful for the generous help of Achmad Suaedy, Andrew Trigg, Bill Shepard, Bob Hefner, Carool Kersten, David May, Djohan Effendi, Emran Qureshi, Fanou Filali, Ibrahim M. Abu-Rabi, Jaap Timmer, Judith Fergin, Maria Ressa, Sarah Ferguson, Sidney Jones, Simon Philpott, Syafi'i Anwar, Vedi Hadiz, Zannuba and her dad, and many other friends, and the quiet encouragement of my parents, Jim and Edie, in developing this book. I am also grateful for the encouragement of Peter Browne and Julian Thomas and the skilful editorial assistance of Carla Taines that ensured that it finally saw the light of day.

This small book grew out of writing and research commenced in early 2002 but it builds on research on Islam in Indonesia first begun in 1988. This research has benefited considerably over the last decade from the support of the Australian Research Council through research grants to study Islam in Indonesia, and of my employer, Deakin University, in allowing me to spend dozens of months on field research in Indonesia. I am grateful to both institutions for their support. Very often my field trips would not have been possible without the assistance of my colleagues who covered my teaching commitments in my absence and I am thankful for their collegiality and help, and in particular for the support and friendship of Ian Weeks.

Although only appearing now in this third paragraph, always at the top of my list are Siew Mee and Hannah. They endured my frequent absences from home and, even when at home, from their company, and have graciously accepted that a large part of our "leisure time" is given over to my research and writing (if I were to spend but the barest amount of time in research and writing the weeks would still be very full with teaching, course development and administration).

I am also grateful to the many Indonesians who have generously given of their time, hospitality and knowledge in helping me, bit by bit, to understand Indonesian and Muslim society a little better. Indonesian–Australian relations are often described as being problematic. My own experience as a Christian Australian in Muslim Indonesia is that people-to-people relations between our two nations are, on the whole, exceptionally good and I deeply appreciate all that Indonesia and the people of Indonesia have given me.

— *Greg Barton, August 2004*